J5 /620

THE HARMONIUM HANDBOOK

"... a welcome
manual and important resource
for music scholars and followers of spiritual
paths alike. This book is a treasure."
—HENRY DOKTORSKI, Founder, The Classical
Free-Reed Company, and author,
The Classical Squeezebox

D1585791

LV 21550360

Liverpool Libraries

THE HARMONIUM HANDBOOK

*Owning, Playing, & Maintaining the
Devotional Instrument of India*

SATYAKI KRAIG BROCKSCHMIDT

New Age Books

ISBN: 81-7822-213-2

First Indian Edition: Delhi, 2004

(First published by Crystal Clarity Publishers, 14618 Tyler Foote Road,
Nevada City, California 95959; Tel.: 530-478-7600)

© 2003 by Kraig Brockschmidt

All rights reserved. No part of this publication may be reproduced
or transmitted in any form or by any means, electronic or mechanical,
including photocopying, recording, or by any information storage and
retrieval system, without permission in writing from the publishers.

Published by
NEW AGE BOOKS
A-44 Naraina Phase-I
New Delhi-110 028 (INDIA)
Email: nab@vsnl.in
Website: www.newagebooksindia.com

For Sale in Indian Subcontinent Only

Printed in India
at Shri Jainendra Press
A-45 Naraina Phase-I, New Delhi-110 028

For devotees of all faiths,
in all lands.

ACKNOWLEDGMENTS

This book began with a loose-leaf set of use and repair instructions written by David & Asha Praver (Palo Alto, CA) specifically for Bina Model 23B harmoniums. When I began to import other models besides the 23B in 1998, I thought to expand a little on David & Asha's work to include a few details of these additional models. Of course, like many projects this one decided to grow well beyond the original plan: I found myself adding photographs, adding a "how to play" section, adding more details on troubleshooting and repair, and researching the history of the instrument itself. Soon it became clear that an entire book was happening. So here it is!

In my historical research, I'm grateful to harmonium enthusiasts Henry Doktorski, Carl Shannon, Joop Rodenburg, and Ian Robertson for their kind help. I'd also like to thank John Schlenck and Sister Gargi at the Vedanta Society in New York for answering my questions regarding Swami Vivekananda and the harmonium.

Where technical questions are concerned, the good folks at Bina Musical Instruments in Delhi, India, have always been happy to provide answers.

My deepest gratitude goes to those who took the time to review various drafts of this handbook and to offer many valuable improvements: Savitri Simpson, Durga Smallen, Stewart Motyka, Jeanne Tchantz, Asha Praver, Terry and Padma McGilloway, Shivani Lucki, and Kristy Dewey. Thanks also to Peter (Dharmadas) Schuppe, Willow Kushler, and Susan McGinnis for help with layout and design, and to Sean Meshorer at Crystal Clarity, Publishers who was enthusiastic about this book from the moment he saw it.

Thanks finally to my wife, Kristi (a.k.a. Iswari) for her never-ending support and encouragement, as well as a number of helpful improvements to this work.

CONTENTS

PHOTO CREDITS

Figure 1-1: Randy-Raine Reusch, courtesy of Henry Doktorski and the Classical Free-Reed, Inc. Web site, http://trfn.clpgh.org/free-reed/

Figure 1-2: From *Zhongguo Gu Wenming [Ancient Chinese Civilization]* (Taipei: Hankun wenhua shiye youxian gongsi, 1983), 51, courtesy of Dr. Ping Yao, California State University, Los Angeles. This *shêng* came from a tomb excavated in 1978 in what is now Hubei Province. Inscriptions on the bronzes found at the site identify the tomb as that of Marquis Yi of the state of Zeng in the early Warring States period around 430 B.C.

Figure 1-3: Carl Shannon, Pennsylvania

Figure 1-4: By the author

Figures 1-5, 1-6, 1-7: Unknown photographers, courtesy of Joop Rodenburg's Reed Organ Society Web site, http://occ.globalknowledge.net/ros/

Figure 1-8: Unknown photographer, courtesy of the Keyboard Museum, http://www.keyboardmuseum.com

Figure 1-9: Unknown photographer, courtesy of Dwarkin & Sons, Calcutta, India

Figures 1-10: Public domain photograph courtesy of Ananda Church of Self-Realization, Seattle, Washington

All remaining figures in Chapters 2, 3, 4 and 5 by the author with the exception of Figure 2-10, courtesy of Bina Musical Stores, Delhi, India

CHAPTER ONE

A Short History of the Indian Harmonium

In many ways, the harmonium is something of a cross-cultural ambassador of beautiful music and international cooperation. Today the instrument is manufactured almost exclusively in India and is widely used in Indian music. But you might notice that it's a little different from other Indian instruments: unlike the vina, sitar, an so on, it has only a twelve-note scale—just like its Western cousins—and it has a distinctly Western-style keyboard. This might seem a bit off until you understand that the harmonium was originally a Western instrument...sort of. In its present form, you see, it was actually born in the East before coming to the West, and though its parents were Western, their ancestors originally came from the East.

In other words, the harmonium's history has been something of a round-the-world journey, one that does indeed begin in the land of many ancestors: China.

Ancient Asian Origins

Harmoniums, along with the accordion, harmonica, concertina, and a number of others, belong to the family of *free-reed* instruments. These instruments all produce sound through the vibration of one end of a flexible reed while the other end remains fixed. This is distinct from *beating-reed* instruments, such as the clarinet, oboe, and bassoon, wherein sound comes from the impact of the reed against some other surface.

For a simple free-reed demonstration, place a common plastic ruler on the top of a straight-edge table with about a third of the ruler extending over the edge. Firmly hold the ruler against the table with one hand just behind the edge (to prevent it from bouncing), then pluck the free end of the ruler with the other hand. This causes the ruler to vibrate at a particular pitch—a crude sound, yes, but it demonstrates the principle. To change the pitch, lengthen or shorten the free end of the ruler—with a little practice you can learn to pluck out a simple melody, or even create a musical notation based on inches or millimeters!

To explore the roots of this free-reed family tree, we must venture back in time to ancient China and an instrument called the *naw*. Here bamboo reeds were mounted inside a couple of pipes that were in turn attached to a gourd (Figure 1-1). Of course, as one might expect from a musically sophisticated people, the *naw* gradually evolved over centuries into an instrument known as the *shêng*—pronounced "sung," literally "sublime voice"—having anywhere from thirteen to twenty-four pipes (Figure 1-2). Interestingly, it is played not by blowing but rather by sucking air through the mouthpiece while closing off holes near the base of each pipe. This draws air

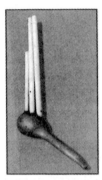

Figure 1-1: A *naw*

through the length of the pipe, causing the reed to vibrate.

No one is sure when the *shêng* was actually invented. Oral traditions place it at 3000 B.C.; others give credit to emperor Huang Tei around 2500 B.C., or to some other unknown innovator around the twelfth century B.C. A very old instrument in any case!

In *The Harmonica: A Mouthful of Music*, Richard Martin describes another primitive mouth-organ of China that resembled (and perhaps even pre-

Figure 1-2: A shêng excavated from the tomb of Marquis Yi, circa 430 B.C.

dated) the *shêng*. This mouth organ used copper reeds instead of bamboo which, according to Martin, "were tuned with blobs of wax" to weigh down the reeds according to pitch. Ancient though this technique may be, it is yet a perfectly legitimate method for tuning modern free-reed instruments such as the harmonium (see Chapter Five).

European and American Reed Organs

In Asia, many varieties of mouth organs followed the *shêng*: the Philippine *kobing*, the Japanese *Sho* (or *Shou*), and the Burmese *hnyin*, to name a few. The *shêng* also gave rise to other reed instruments such as the Indian *shehnai* and the Chinese *sona*.

In the West, it is suspected that the *shêng* or one of its descendents was brought back to Europe around the thirteenth century by Marco Polo, or maybe it was migrating Tartars out of Russia—we don't really know. We can at least be certain that it was known by the early seventeeth century, and that many more examples likely found their way West in the hands of travelers and missionaries over the next hundred-plus years.

Many Europeans were deeply interested by the *shêng* and its free-reed progeny because these little mouth organs held the promise to fulfill a long-sought desire. As Arthur W. J. G. Ord-Hume writes in his delightful book, *Harmonium: The History of the Reed Organ and its Makers*:

> The sustained tone of the organ pipe had already been known and appreciated for over 2,000 years, and the organ itself offered an advantage over plucked keyboard string instruments. Coveted as organ-tone was, however, the large and expensive pipe organ remained out of the reach of the musical majority.[*]

---

[*]Davis & Charles Publishers, London, 1986, page 13.

11

It's no surprise, then, that with all these Asian issues floating around, a number of distinctly European free-reed instruments began to appear by the late eighteenth century. Some of these, like the harmonica, were small mouth organs like their Asiatic counterparts; others grew into handheld or free-standing instruments with various sorts of keyboards and air-pumping devices.

The most notable of these, from the standpoint of this book, was a free-reed organ built by a man named Kirschnik, sometime around 1770. "Kirschnik's Harmonica," as it was called, had an organ-style keyboard played with the right hand and a rear bellows pumped with the left hand—the same basic design as today's Indian harmoniums!

However, Kirschnik's Harmonica was probably a little ahead of its time, and perhaps too simple. For whatever reason, it didn't really catch on. Yet it served as the inspiration for many grander variations as befit the imperial ambitions of the age. Having seen Kirschnik's design, one Georg Joseph Vogler commissioned a Swedish master builder named Rakwitz (who had, in fact, been Kirschnik's assistant) to construct a larger reed organ. This instrument, called "Volger's Orchestrion"—even the name sounds majestic!—was completed in 1790 and reportedly had four keyboards (or "manuals") of sixty-three notes each plus a pedalboard of thirty-nine notes.

From then on into the nineteenth century, experimentation was widespread both technically and geographically. Many a savvy inventor clearly saw the massive market potential for a simple and affordable reed organ. Or, to put it in the modern vernacular, finding a workable design was "all the rage."

Doubtless inspired by the Orchestrion, scores of different reed-organs quickly appeared on the scene with fabulous names such as the Pansymphonicon, Uranion, Poikilorgue, Royal Seraphine, and Aeolo-melodicon. And with all this experimentation going on, "the world was poised," as Ord-Hume explains, "for the invention that would act as a catalyst and produce the definitive instrument" (p. 24).

That invention came through Frenchman Alexandre Debain, who in 1842 patented a reed-organ design called the "Harmonium." This design became the reference point for nearly everything that followed—and did it follow! The reed-organ industry, with hundreds of manufacturers, not only blossomed in Europe but also reached across the Atlantic to the United States. There was so much interest, in fact, that by the second half of the nineteenth century, writes Henry Doktorski,

> The harmonium had evolved into a sophisticated instrument. The bellows were pumped by two foot pedals and the more expensive models had two keyboard manuals (each encompassing a range of five octaves) with up to thirteen stops...including tremolo and one or two knee-pedals to control volume. It was a popular instrument for churches which could not afford a pipe organ. In addition, it was favored for home music-making alongside the piano and in the cinema as a means of musical illustration in the era before sound films. Many nineteenth-century composers [e.g. Rossini, Saint-Saëns, Dvořák, and Reger] wrote serious music for the harmonium.*

In Figure 1-3, you can see a number of classical nineteenth century harmoniums with their full keyboards, abundant stop-knobs, and foot pedal pumps. Many such instruments, like the one in Figure 1-4, became a central piece of furniture in many Victorian homes, oftentimes acting as a type of hutch with platforms on either side of the keyboard to hold vases of flowers (or swans, as the case may be).

Indeed, as the harmonium caught the popular fancy, manufacturers introduced increasingly ornate models over the years. Some even had rows of gilded pipes to make the

---

*From a forthcoming book by Henry Doktorski, *The Classical Sqeezebox: A History of Free-Reed Instruments in Classical Music.*

instrument look like a big organ. Of course, none of those pipes had any effect whatsoever on the instrument's sound. Likewise, you can imagine what harmonium makers did when popular opinion held that a harmonium's overall weight and number of stop-knobs were the most important measures of quality!

Figure 1-3: Several classical harmoniums of the nineteenth century

Figure 1-4: Many Victorian homes included a harmonium. This one graces the parlor of the Black Swan Inn, Tilton, New Hampshire.

Though it took some time for the harmonium to be considered a "real" instrument by the musical purists of the age, it was immensely popular in the home. As Ord-Hume writes:

> For the small working-class home where pretentions were limited by reality, the reed organ was acceptable in every respect and, in times more godly than ours today, there was a certain added benefit in owning an instrument which could be used to play religious music with some of the timbre of the chapel organ. Indeed, ownership of a harmonium could be justified to the piano-conscious snob on the grounds of its being a devotional instrument. Remember that hymns were very frequently sung, not just on Sundays, also that many of the popular pieces of drawing-room music tended towards the languorous and the bathetic. The popular reed organ thus found instant acceptance with a very large sector of the public. (p. 86)

Even when electric organs began to appear, the harmonium remained popular in the home for the simple fact that electricity, well into the twentieth century, was a luxury that many homes did not enjoy. Harmoniums, in fact, continued to serve in the field as late as the Korean War (Figures 1-5, 1-6, and 1-7).

Figure 1-5: 1905 postcard from Camp Northfield, Massachusetts

Figure 1-6: Harmonium in use at sea during World War II,
played by the seated sailor on the left (May 18th, 1944)

Yet starting in the last quarter of the nineteenth century, it was electricity and all things technological that now caught the West's fancy, even where music was concerned. In 1876, Elisha Gray—who would have been remembered as the inventor of the telephone if he hadn't gotten to the patent office an hour later than Alexander Graham Bell—invented one of the very first electronic musical instruments. His "Musical Telegraph" (a by-

Figure 1-7: Harmonium in use by the U.S. Army in Korea

product of his work on the telephone—see Figure 1-8) employed reeds whose vibrations were controlled by electromagnets rather than air, vibrations that could then be either amplified or transmitted over a wire. The inventor of the vacuum tube, Lee De Forest, also recognized the musical potential of his

Figure 1-8: Elisha Gray's "Musical Telegraph"

creation. In 1915, he produced the "Audion Piano," precursor to today's electronic keyboards, that was capable of reproducing the sounds of a variety of instruments, not only the organ. And two decades later, the wildly popular Hammond Organ appeared on the scene, literally setting the "tone" for just about everything since, whether built with tubes, transistors, or digital circuitry.

Thus it was that "old-fashioned" instruments such as the harmonium became increasingly *blasé*, and the once-booming industry fell into rapid decline. By the 1940s, harmoniums were no longer manufactured in the West at all. (It's ironic that today's digital keyboards often synthesize sounds using audio samples from none other than the best old-fashioned pipe and reed organs.)

In *The New Grove Dictionary of Music and Musicians*, Alfred Berner perhaps gives the best summary of what happened to this once-beloved instrument:

> The decline of interest, which began about 1930, was due to a change in musical taste. Music in the home as well as musical education in general turned increasingly away from the musical style of the 19th century. The harmonium and everything connected with it fell under the heading of "kitsch." Even in light music it was ousted by its more wieldy cousin, the accordion. Above all, however, with the advent of a whole range of electronic instruments, rival

17

instruments have appeared which not only far surpass the sound combinations and expressive possibilities of the harmonium as a solo or accompanying instrument, but match completely the world of modern musical sounds. In sacred music, where the harmonium...had taken the place of the organ, it has in its turn been replaced by either a small portable organ or an electronic organ. Just when the harmonium had reached its peak technically it became musically redundant and was laid aside.*

Laid aside in the West, perhaps, but not everywhere...

(Re)Invention of the Indian Harmonium

In the same way that the harmonium was an excellent substitute for a pipe organ in small churches that could not afford the latter, it was also better suited for travel and for use in venues where electricity was not readily available.

In the mid-nineteenth century, Christian missionaries were among those who traveled to various parts of the world with harmoniums in their hands and hymns on their lips. For those who ventured to China, India, and other Asian lands, little did they realize that they were bringing the harmonium to its ancestral homeland! It is not surprising, then, that while Christianity itself didn't necessarily flourish in the Orient to the degree hoped for by the missionaries, the harmonium did.

This was especially true in India, where devotional music is so much an integral aspect of daily life. However, the typically large European harmoniums were not very well suited to the Indian lifestyle. For one, they required a chair—considered wholly superfluous in many nineteenth-century Indian homes. Second, harmoniums were somewhat fragile, their complex internal mechanisms being rather prone to failure in the environmental extremes of the

---

*Quoted in *The Classical Harmonium* by Henry Doktorski, http://trfn.clpgh.org/free-reed/history/harmonium.html.

subcontinent. Third, by Indian standards of "portability"—which often requires playing an instrument in a strolling procession!—European harmoniums were very large and ungainly. And fourth, all but the smallest harmoniums created an artificial barrier between the person playing it and those for whom it was being played, especially if the instrument was positioned against a wall as many were designed to be. In a land that treasures intimate *satsang* (fellowship with like-minded souls) and the devotional *kirtan* (group singing/chanting, often done in procession), the common European design just didn't work all that well.

Figure 1-9:
Dwarkanath
(Dwarka) Ghose

Yet there were other, less popular designs that held much more promise for the Indians, namely certain "miniature" or "portable" harmoniums that had been developed along the lines of Kirschnik's Harmonica; doubtless some examples also made their way East with their more unwieldy siblings. It was probably one of these that inspired a Calcutta resident by the name of Dwarkanath (Dwarka) Ghose (Figure 1-9) to produce a homegrown harmonium more suited to his countrymen.

The year was 1875, only one year before Elisha Gray's original electronic keyboard. After much experimentation, Dwarka developed simplified designs for the reed board, the keyboard mechanism, and the bellows, making them less expensive to build and easier to repair. His instrument was also specifically designed to be played while seated on the floor: one hand on the keyboard, the other on the bellows. After all, one only needs two hands to play complex chords...Indian music, which emphasizes melody, has no chords. Instead, much Indian music often employs a continuous "drone" of some sort as an accompaniment. For this purpose, Dwarka also added the uniquely Indian drone reeds that don't exist in Western models.

Dwarka certainly struck a chord (to what extent they exist!) in the Indian consciousness. His design has, in a sense, revolutionized Indian music, wherein the harmonium is employed in nearly every style and genre save the classical forms of southern India. Just as harmoniums were once popular in Europe and America for devotional music, so harmoniums remain widely popular in India to this day—especially seeing as how electricity in India is still either wholly unavailable or wholly unreliable. And while harmonium manufacturing is completely extinct in the West, the industry is alive and well in India.

Coming Full Circle

Thus, from Kirschnik's original hand-pumped "harmonica" of 1770, the Western harmonium had grown into a large foot-pumped instrument only to become obsolete at the hands of its own electronic offspring. It seems appropriate, then, that the various hand-pumped designs that hardly made it off the ground, so to speak, found new life in a land where most people still sit on the floor and where devotion is still valued more than technology. And interestingly enough, it is from that land that the harmonium has returned to become increasingly popular in the West once again.

In 1920, just about when the grand, free-standing harmoniums began their free-fall in the West, a young man later known to the world as Paramhansa Yogananda (Figure 1-10, next page)—and author of the spiritual classic *Autobiography of a Yogi*—sailed from his Calcutta home to take up permanent residence in the United States. His purpose was to facilitate a broad and harmonious exchange of ideals—both material and spiritual—between East and West, especially as new forms of transportation and communication were beginning to "shrink" the world at a rapid pace. And likely stowed with the rest of his luggage was a new-style Indian harmonium, which he re-

Figure 1-10: Paramhansa
Yogananda in the 1920's

introduced to Americans along with the Eastern forms of devotional chanting, suitably adapted and translated to better fit the Western ear.*

Since then, Eastern-style devotional chanting and other musical forms have certainly become increasingly popular in America and Europe, especially as Eastern teachings, in general, have become more widely accepted.

Fundamental to these teachings—including those of Yogananda as well as his predecessor in the United States, Swami Vivekananda, the revered disciple of Sri Ramakrishna—is the understanding that beneath their outward forms, all religions and cultural traditions share an underlying unity, and that there is real benefit in drawing the best out of each.

Thus in the humble Indian harmonium we find a symbol of a new and important understanding. For as the instrument is itself a balanced blend of East and West, and as its individual reeds combine to produce beautiful music, may we too, as individuals of all faiths and all lands, join together in loving, *harmonious* cooperation for the upliftment of all humankind.

---

*That he was successful in this effort is attested to by his singing *O God Beautiful* (his translation of a perennial favorite of the medieval saint Guru Nanak, founder of the Sikh order), for nearly and hour and a half with a crowd of 3,000 in Carnegie Hall, New York, in 1925. The story is told in his autobiography.

21

For Further Study

Recommended historical reading includes *The American Reed Organ and the Harmonium,* by Robert F. Gellerman, and *Harmonium: The History of the Reed Organ and its Makers,* by Arthur W. J. G. Ord-Hume. On the Web, try Henry Doktorski's Classical Free Reed, Inc. site, http://trfn.clpgh.org/free-reed/main.html. For an excellent history of electronic instruments see http://www.obsolete.com/120_years/.

On the subject of chanting, see Yogananda's *Cosmic Chants,* Self-Realization Fellowship, Los Angeles, CA, as well as both *Awaken to Superconsciousness* and *The Art and Science of Raja Yoga,* by J. Donald Walters (Swami Kriyananda), Crystal Clarity Publishers, Nevada City, CA.

CHAPTER TWO

To Know and Love Your Harmonium: A User's Guide

By and large, harmoniums need only a little care to keep them beautiful on the outside and melodious on the inside for many years. As we'll see in this chapter, harmoniums are not terribly complex, and knowing more about how they work is helpful in getting the most out of them.

Nearly all Indian harmoniums, no matter their size or any other external features, share a few elements in common: a keyboard, an external bellows on the back, a lock, some number of knobs on the front, and some kind of case that holds it all together (Figure 2-1). Depending on the manufacturer and the particular whims of their craftsmen, certain bits may or may not be present. The cover glass, for instance, might be all wood instead of glass; small hinges

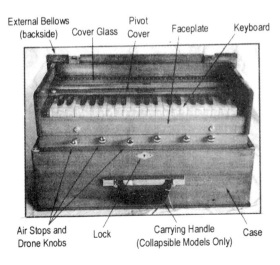

Figure 2-1: Primary harmonium features (collapsible model shown)

that are commonly hidden behind the faceplate might be attached on the outside instead.

Standard harmoniums have carrying handles on the sides and a wooden cover that slips onto the top (Figure 2-2). The cover should be fairly self-explanatory; do note, however, that it slides onto the top horizontally rather than being set down vertically. Small metal brackets on the back corners of the harmonium (Figure 2-3) fit into slots on the cover and hold it in place.

Carrying Handles (on side) Top Cover

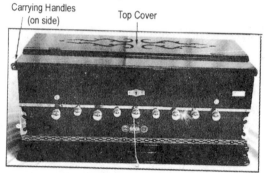

Figure 2-2: Standard harmonium with cover in place

Figure 2-3: Corner brackets on a standard harmonium

Collapsible harmoniums[*] (as in Figure 2-1), fold down into a smaller box (Figure 2-4) and are carried by the handle like a suitcase. Specific instructions for opening and closing such an instrument are given later in this chapter.

With your harmonium you might have a weak excuse for a key, dangling on a similar excuse for a string, that fits into what a might generously be called a "lock" (see Figure 2-1). Let me be blunt: make sure the harmonium is

[*]Sometimes called "portable" harmoniums, but this is a misnomer because all Indian harmoniums are rather portable, especially compared with their classical Western brethren.

Figure 2-4: Fully closed collapsible harmonium

unlocked then *throw the key away*. They key and lock are rather flimsy and can easily break; not a good thing if this happens when the instrument is closed up. There's almost no reason to use the key anyway if you keep the instrument away from curious young children and gorillas, so you might as well save yourself the trouble and remove the key from your consciousness entirely.

We'll now take a closer look at the various parts of the harmonium and how they work. While it's not necessary to understand these details in order to play the harmonium, they can very much help you understand how to play the harmonium *well*. Like all instruments, harmoniums have their special quirks.

Keyboard

The harmonium keyboard is likely a familiar sight since it looks like any other black-and-white Western-style keyboard. Harmonium keyboards come in two styles: *piano style* (Figure 2-5a), wherein the keys have squared ends, and *organ style* (Figure 2-5b), with rounded ends that extend out a little.

Figures 2-5a, 2-5b: Piano style keys (left) and organ style keys (right)

In either case, the harmonium plays much more like an organ than a piano, primarily in that how hard you press a key has relatively little effect on the volume or timbre (quality) of the resulting sound (compared with how you pump the bellows, as described in Chapter Three, pages 47–51). A practical upshot of this is that you can be gentle and smooth when playing a harmonium: there is no need to pound the keyboard like those classical pianists who had reputations for destroying even the most robust issues from the master artisans of Europe. In other words, it's entirely possible to break the keys with too much force. So play nice, like Mother always said!

Most harmoniums are built around a C scale, with C being the lowest (leftmost) note. (Only some "classical" harmoniums manufactured in the nineteenth to early twentieth century were built around an F scale instead.) On C-scale harmoniums, the lowest note is one octave below middle C (Figure 2-6). Depending on your model, there will then be anywhere from 2½ to 3½ (or more) octaves as you move up the scale to the right. A 2½ octave keyboard will end a few notes above "High C" in the figure; a 3½-octave (or larger) keyboard will extend a few more keys above "Really High C."

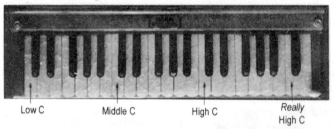

Low C   Middle C   High C   Really
High C

Figure 2-6: A common 3¼ octave C-scale harmonium keyboard

The keys are specially shaped pieces that are cut from a single block of wood, thereby ensuring that they all fit together nicely. Some kind of plastic or nylon is then glued to the tops of the keys; the white keys also get a piece of the same material on the front, while the black keys are painted on the sides.

Chapter Four will delve into the details of inner keyboard mechanisms for curious readers, but one effect of the mechanics is important to note here. While the keys are designed primarily to move up and down, they usually have a little horizontal and rotational play from side to side. Normally this is not a problem. However, if you push or pull a key to one side while the adjacent key is down, you may find that the first key doesn't pop up when you release it because of sideways friction from the second key. Sometimes a particular key will have more play than usual and will therefore appear to stick more often than others. If you encounter this, fear not! Adjustments can be made—either mechanically or in one's playing style!—to appropriately limit the key's motion.

Bellows

The bellows are the breathing diaphragm of the harmonium, invariably located on the back side of the instrument where they can be pumped with either the left or the right hand while the other hand plays the keyboard.

Bellows come in two different styles. *Top-fold* bellows (Figure 2-7, also called *double-fold* or *triple-fold* bellows) are hinged at the bottom so the whole top edge moves in and out. Top-pumping bellows are released by a single latch located midway along the top edge or by two latches on either end. They auto-

Latch

Figure 2-7: Open top-fold bellows

27

matically open up (as shown in the picture) thanks to a little torsion rod that runs between the bottom middle of the bellows and one side of the harmonium's case. Without this rod, you'd have to manually push the bellows out each time before pulling them in again.

Side-fold bellows (Figure 2-8, also called *multi-fold* bellows) have vertical hinges on both sides that also dou-

Latch

ble as latches. Side-fold bellows are released by swinging *one* of these two pivot latches aside (Figure 2-8). This means you can open the bellows on either side, depending on the hand you use for pumping (typically the left.) Don't release both sides at once, however, or your bellows will be hanging limply from the back of the harmonium with no hinge point whatsoever!

Figure 2-8: Open side-fold bellows

Side-fold bellows also open automatically thanks to a spiral spring that's located *inside* the bellows themselves. If you want the bellows to pop open farther than they do, you can remove the valve cover on the back of the bellows, remove the spring, stretch it open a little more, and reassemble everything.

One Bellows or Two?

The quality of sound produced by a harmonium depends in large part on having a reasonably constant air flow passing through the instrument throughout any given performance. For this purpose, all harmoniums actually have a *second* bellows that is typically hidden inside the case, along with some way for air to move in and out of the case itself. (Standard harmoniums have holes on the back side underneath the external bellows; collapsible harmoniums have a gap between the upper part and the case.)

The internal bellows serve as a buffer for the air brought in by the external bellows. In most harmonium designs, the internal bellows are horizontally positioned inside the instrument's case, underneath the reed chamber, and are never visible. In some designs, like the "Dulcetina" (Figure 2-9), the "internal" bellows are located on the front of the instrument, where you can actually see their buffering operation. It is quite instructive to watch a Dulcetina in action.

Figure 2-9: A "Dulcetina" harmonium

The two bellows work in tandem through a pair of one-way valves; for more details of the mechanisms involved, see Chapter Four (page 91). For now, it's sufficient to say that when you pump the external bellows, air pressure builds inside the internal bellows, pressure that is not allowed to escape except through the reeds. When you depress one or more keys, this pressure is gradually released through the corresponding reeds, causing them to vibrate. One or more springs attached to the internal bellows help the process along, gradually squeezing out all the air. This is why the harmonium continues to produce sound for a time after you stop pumping the external bellows.

With this two-bellows design, you shouldn't pump the external bellows more than two or three times without having at least one air stop open and at least one key depressed. Otherwise you will build up pressure inside either bellows, possibly causing one or the other to spring a leak. When this happens, the harmonium won't be able to sustain a good sound and becomes what is lovingly called a "wheezer."

When closing and latching the bellows, always depress some keys to allow all internal air to escape. This is especially important with collapsible harmoniums because collapsing compresses both the external and internal bellows to their fullest extent. Any residual pressure in the internal bellows would thus increase, possibly damaging them.

It's also good to periodically take a small paintbrush or toothbrush and clean out any dust and other particular matter that might have accumulated in the folds of the external bellows. This material can eventually form lumps that might damage the bellows when you close them.

Stops and Drones

Depending on the model and manufacturer, an Indian harmonium will have any where from zero to as many as nine or ten knobs sticking out of the front of the case. For specific details of common Bina harmonium models, see Appendix A (page 125). Generally speaking, however, each knob serves one of three purposes: air stops, drones, and the tremolo.

AIR STOP KNOBS

Air stop knobs open holes between the internal bellows and a specific reed chamber, allowing air to pass through those reeds when keys are depressed. *Double-reed* harmoniums typically have a *bass* set of reeds (low register) and a *male* set (middle register); *triple-reed* harmoniums add a *female* set (high register). Each set of reeds will sound only if at least one air stop is open for that particular set; the more stops you have open for a particular set, the more air you allow to flow past those reeds.

These air stops are not all-or-nothing propositions: each stop can be opened only partway. This, along with there possibly being more than one stop per set of reeds on your particular harmonium, allows you to finely adjust the volume of the reed sets relative to one another. So if you want more of one register, you can open additional stops for that one or partially close stops for the other registers. Whenever you start to work with a new harmonium, it's well worth a little experimentation to see how each air stop affects the overall sound. (It's also fun to have a friend play the instrument while you fiddle with the stops.)

Do note, however, that some instruments lack a good seal between the reed chambers such that the different sets are not isolated. In these cases, you won't hear much difference between the air stops.

DRONE KNOBS

With at least one air stop open (typically for the male set or the tremolo), these knobs activate special *drone reeds* (visible in Figure 2-11) that produce sound independently of the keyboard. Drone reeds are usually thicker than the other reeds in the harmonium and thus produce a slightly different and somewhat softer sound. This means that you can't really hear them much over other notes you play on the keyboard. Still, if used sensitively they can add a certain depth to particular songs.

In most Indian harmoniums, the specific drone notes (however many) correspond to the black keys (flats/sharps) on the keyboard: $D^b/C^\#$, $E^b/D^\#$, $G^b/F^\#$, $A^b/G^\#$, and $B^b/A^\#$. This means that unless you're playing a piece in an appropriate key and/or primarily with chords that include the specific notes in question, the built-in drones on your harmonium may or may not be all that useful to you. Furthermore, you can use any note on the keyboard as a drone, as befits the song being played (see Chapter Three, page 59). So there's no need to feel guilty if you never use the built-in drones.

HINT: You can also simulate a drone with any given key by removing the cover glass (or wood, if that's the case) and gently moving the little metal spring on that key to an adjacent key (Figure 2-10). This will cause the key to stay down, thereby producing a continuous sound.

Figure 2-10: Creating a drone by moving a key spring (left)

THE TREMOLO KNOB

This knob (there is only ever one) activates a fascinating mechanism for one set of reeds, provided no other air stops are open for that set. This special feature is a carry-over from the original Western classical harmoniums in which various manufacturers tried all sorts of ingenious methods to produce a *vibrato* effect.[*]

The particular mechanism that continues to be built into most Indian harmoniums is perhaps the least sophisticated of them all—it consists of a flap of leather that is glued down on one edge of a stop block. This flap covers

---

[*]These are described in Robert Gellerman's *The American Reed Organ and the Harmonium* and include rotating paper fans and little hammers that bounced against the reeds.

an air hole (through the block) from the internal bellows to one of the reed chambers (Figure 2-11). A small block of wood is glued to the top of this flap to weigh it down. When the tremolo knob is pulled out—and again, it works only if no other air stops are open—the air pressure from the internal bellows pushes the weighted flap up, allowing air to flow past the reeds as you play. However, the flap and its little weight naturally want to snap back down; when they do so, they momentarily stop the flow of air and thus stop the sound. Of course, the air pressure will immediately open the flap up again, resuming the sound, only to have it momentarily stopped again.

Figure 2-11: A typical tremolo in an Indian harmonium. Notice the two drone reeds on the right and the shafts leading to the external knobs.

As intriguing as this mechanism is, the resulting sound is—in short—a kind of, well, flapping warble that you probably won't want to use unless you're playing "Amazing Grace" at some excessively mawkish funeral. To make it even more fun, the rate of flapping changes with pressure: it slows down if you depress more keys and speeds up if you depress fewer. It also runs a little faster for high notes and slower for low notes (as the air flow differs between them). Personally, I don't know of anyone who actually uses this feature; my guess is that you'll probably exclude it from your own personal devotions.

Besides, the tremolo is not always reliable; in some harmoniums it never really gets going. In the worst case, it simply acts more or less like a weak air stop.[*]

---

[*]People sometimes play a common six-knob collapsible harmonium with the first, third, and fifth knobs pulled out. The first and third knobs open

Which Knob Does What?

Occasionally one comes across a harmonium with no knobs on the front at all. In this case, it's easy to answer this question: air is always allowed to flow to all the reeds, and there are no drone notes and no tremolo.

Most harmoniums, though, have at least two knobs for the air stops, at least one drone, and a tremolo. As for which knobs serve which purpose—well, this varies among different manufacturers, among different models from the same manufacturer, and even occasionally between two instances of the same model from the same manufacturer! (Again, see Appendix A, page 125, for typical Bina configurations.) Some models have smaller knobs for the drones and larger ones for the air stops and the tremolo, but oftentimes the knobs will all be the same size with no identifying marks whatsoever.

Hopefully your harmonium came with some information about its exact arrangement. If not, the sure-fire way to find out is to open up the harmonium and take a look inside, as we'll see in Chapter Four. The other option— which is less exacting, mind you, is to simply fiddle around with the knobs and see what they do. If, in your fiddling, you are holding down a key and pumping the bellows and not getting any sound, STOP—you probably don't have any air stops open at all. As I cautioned earlier, too much pumping without making a sound can damage the bellows.

Another caution is to avoid twisting the knobs too much in one direction or the other. By "too much," I mean something on the order of two or more full rotations. This is not a problem for normal people—it's only an issue for those of us who might be described as "categorical fiddlers." This caution, in other words, comes from personal

---

stops for both male and bass reed sets; the fifth, however, is the tremolo knob and doesn't do anything with the other two open.

experience. If you turn too much counter-clockwise, you can unscrew the knob from whatever internal mechanism it's connected to. Too much clockwise rotation can effectively pull the stop out partway, even when the knob itself is fully pushed in.

Coupler

Some harmoniums are fitted with another interesting mechanism called a *coupler*, which, like the tremolo, is carried over from classical Western designs. A coupler effectively connects one key with its counterpart either an octave above (a *super-octave* coupler) or an octave below (a *sub-octave* coupler). The net result of this is that you double the number of reeds involved, thereby making the sound more "full" or "grand." It also more or less doubles the air flow needed to maintain a particular volume, which becomes somewhat difficult if you're playing chords.

The coupler on Bina harmoniums consists of a small lever located on the right side of the keyboard (Figure 2-12). The coupler is typically engaged when the lever is pushed back and disengaged when the lever is pulled forward. Other manufacturers employ a separate, distinct knob for the coupler wherein pushing or pulling the knob engages the mechanism.

Figure 2-12: Engaged Bina coupler lever; to disengage, pull the lever toward the front.

35

Opening and Closing
a Collapsible Harmonium

If you are working with a collapsible harmonium, you should know a few things about opening and closing the instrument, as described here.

OPENING

1. Place the harmonium bottom down (as in Figure 2-4, page 25) and undo the lid latches on both sides (Figure 2-13).

2. Flip the lid over the back, exposing the external bellows (Figure 2-14).

Lid
latch

Release button

Figure 2-13: Location of lid latches and release buttons

Figure 2-14: Flipping
the lid over the back

3. Push in the rectangular release buttons on the sides at the bottom of the case (see Figure 2-13). You may need to push hard, possibly while pushing down a little on the whole keyboard assembly. When you press the buttons in, the keyboard assembly will spring up a little and sit loosely in the case (Figure 2-15).

Figure 2-15: Keyboard assembly after being released.

4. Pull up on both sides of the keyboard assembly until the side latch buttons click out on the top of the case (Figure 2-16). This may be effortless or it might take a little push and pull, depending on the specific instrument. Don't be afraid to exert a little force. You can even set the harmonium on its face for a little "gravitational nullification" (to use the scientific term). In any case, what's important is getting the little silver latch buttons on the sides to click out firmly. These buttons are all that hold up the inner part of the harmonium, to make room inside the case for the internal bellows to move up and down.

Figure 2-16: Latch buttons (left) hold the assembly on top of the case. Bellows latches (right) hold the bellows against the case.

5. Secure the side latches to keep the external bellows snugly connected to the main body of the harmonium (see Figure 2-15). This is important for getting an optimal air flow through the instrument.

6. Pull out the desired stops, let out the bellows, and you are ready to play!

CLOSING

1. **IMPORTANT:** *Ensure that all the air pressure is drained from both bellows* by depressing some keys (or many at once using your forearm) and pulling the external bellows in until you can latch them closed. Keep the keys down for a second or two *after* the sound dies away completely.

2. **ALSO IMPORTANT:** *Push in all the knobs on the front of the instrument.* Otherwise step 4 is considerably difficult.

3. Unlatch the lid/bellows from the main harmonium body and flip it over the top (Figure 2-17).

Figure 2-17: Collapsible harmonium ready to collapse. Make sure the knobs are in!

4. Firmly push in the two side latch buttons (visible in Figure 2-16) which will release the keyboard assembly allowing it to drop into the case (back to the position shown in Figure 2-15). If these buttons are tight, you might need to pull up on the sides of the keyboard assembly with your thumbs and forefingers while reaching down with your middle fingers to press the buttons. In extreme cases a friend can be a tremendous blessing.

5. Firmly press the keyboard assembly down into the case until the release buttons pop out at the bottom (as shown in Figure 2-13). If this doesn't happen perfectly, don't worry—the lid latches will keep the instrument securely shut.

6. Latch the lid to the body (as in Figure 2-13).

As mentioned earlier, don't bother with the lock and key if your harmonium has them. Both are flimsy and might break at an inconvenient time. The instrument is usually quite secure when the lid is latched down.

Dusting and Cleaning

A harmonium's outside appearance has very little to do with the quality of its sound. I once had a 60+-year-old harmonium that had a lovely sound, even though the case was cracked and the varnish on one side had blistered to the point of flaking off.

Nevertheless, most people find it much more enjoyable and inspiring to play a clean, shining instrument than a dirty, dusty, or damaged one. In certain ways, a harmonium's bright appearance adds a subtle brightness to any performance. (Furniture polish, by the way, works fine on a harmonium to give it a little extra shine, if so desired.)

Any piece of lint-free fabric, such as a silk brocade, makes an excellent dust cover when your harmonium is not in use. If you choose to keep it uncovered—presumably because you're playing it often!—do take the time to dust it off every now and then (and clean out the bellows folds, as mentioned on page 30). A slightly damp cloth works well for external cleaning. Pay special attention to all the little horizontal ledges, both front and back; also give extra attention to those keys that you don't play very often—dust is quite invisible against the white keys.

Simple cleaning solutions such as window cleaner or diluted ammonia (20%) work well, especially for cleaning the cover glass. Of course, a cloth will not be able to reach into every little corner; in such places, wrap the cloth around the tip of a toothpick or a slender screwdriver, or simply remove bits of the harmonium's trim as necessary to open up those spaces. This latter option is most useful when you want to clean the corners just above the keyboard; here, just remove the *pivot cover* (Figure 2-18).

Remove two screws and lift off pivot cover.

Figure 2-19: Removing the pivot cover allows detailed cleaning around the keyboard.

Environmental Considerations

Like other wooden instruments, a harmonium is sensitive to variations in temperature and humidity to some degree, although not as much. A guitar, for instance, can easily go out of tune if it sits in the sun or a hot car for an hour; the strings become warm and stretch disproportionately to one another, and the tensile strength of the wood body changes somewhat.

The harmonium, on the other hand, can easily tolerate greater changes without ill effects other than a slight global change in its overall tuning. That is, as temperature increases, all the reeds become more flexible and thus go slightly lower in pitch across the board. As temperature decreases, the reeds become stiffer and thus play slightly higher.

It's an interesting fact that when harmoniums manufactured and tuned in a place such as Delhi, India (hot and humid) come to a cooler clime such as the Pacific Northwest (where I live), they generally seem to be tuned to a standard A of 444 Hz rather than 440 Hz (Hz=Hertz, cycles per second). Yet I've been assured, that each instrument is tuned in the factory to 440 Hz. It seems, then, that a 30°F difference in temperature and a 25 percent difference in humidity could very well effect a 1 percent shift in overall tuning (and even if this isn't the real cause, it at least makes for good discussion...).

All of this is to say that one shouldn't worry too much about using a harmonium in different conditions, or where it sits when not in use. It's perfectly fine to set a harmonium next to an outside wall of your home, for instance, whereas you would generally not do this with a piano (humidity changes play havoc with piano tuning).

Still, prolonged exposure to intense heat sources such as space heaters and sunlight will, over time, cause a harmonium's external finish to deteriorate. Prolonged exposure to sunlight can also cause deterioration and discoloration of the nylon used on the tops of the keys. This, as well as shorter exposure to intense heat (such as a few hours in a hot car) might also cause the nylon to warp and separate from the wooden keys.

Intense temperature changes can also cause one or more reeds within the instrument to make a very annoying buzzing or rattling sound. This is usually caused by some sort of contact between the vibrating reed and the frame to which it's attached. As shown in Figure 5-2 (page 100), there is only a tiny gap (less than a millimeter) between the free end of a reed and the frame—large temperature changes can shrink, expand, or warp either the frame or the reed such that they contact one other.

It is best also to avoid placing the instrument close to a humidifier or a dry air conditioner. This is less a consideration for the reeds than for the harmonium's wood and its leather seals. Too much change in humidity can cause the wood and leather to expand, resulting in keys that stick up or down, air stops that are difficult to move, or difficulty in opening and closing a collapsible harmonium. Too little humidity over a long period of time—and we're talking years here—can also cause the internal leather seals and valves to become brittle, leading to various sorts of air leaks that make the harmonium a real wheezer.

Dust and other airborne particles (such as smoke, salt-water air, and so on) are also long-term concerns for harmonium reeds. Over time—and we're generally talking years again—such particulate matter can accumulate on the reeds themselves. This causes an irregular change in the tuning of individual reeds, making an instrument that is audibly unpleasant.

A case in point is a friend of mine who had a harmonium shipped to California by boat in the mid-1970's. Although the instrument sounded great in India, it had markedly deteriorated by the time it reached American shores. When I had a chance to look at it a few years ago, I found that the reeds had all kinds of corrosion and deposits on them, which presumably began with weeks of exposure to ocean air. As a result, the reeds were randomly out of tune, and the best solution was to replace them entirely. So if your harmonium is regularly exposed to such conditions, you might consider taking the time to thoroughly clean the reeds every few years. This entails the rather tedious chore of removing each individual reed, as described on page 87 in Chapter Four.

Long-Term Storage

As mentioned earlier, a harmonium should ideally be stored away from environmental extremes whether you're actively using it or not. In other words, avoid the hot attic and the musty basement. (I know of one old harmonium that has so much mold on the inside that it literally stinks to play it!) A room-temperature closet is probably the best place. Store the instrument inside its carrying case if you have one. Otherwise, be sure to cover it with breathable fabric; wrapping in a plastic bag is not recommended.

Wherever you store a harmonium, it is a good idea to play it a little every few months (such as when the seasons change) to keep the bellows from becoming too stiff. It's also good to work the knobs in and out a few times to keep them from sticking.

When storing a collapsible harmonium for a long time (many months), it is best to rest it either on the bottom or with the handle side *down*. If it is stored with the handle side up (the obvious way), the leather flap-valve in the external bellows can curl to the point where it won't close properly the next time you play it. This doesn't allow the proper air pressure to build up inside the harmonium, making it—you know the word!—a wheezer. While this condition can be remedied (see Chapter Five, page 112), it's better to avoid it in the first place. If you really must store the instrument handle-side up, you might consider removing this flap entirely and storing it in such a way that it can remain flat.

—Chapter Three—

Playing the Indian Harmonium

Just as the Indian harmonium is unique among musical instruments, playing it well naturally involves a certain set of unique skills. Fortunately, these skills are not terribly difficult, but it will take some practice to develop them.

Pumping the bellows is one such skill, and this is an art form in itself. Another skill comes with the understanding that harmoniums have no sustain capability like a piano, nor do they come with the reverb feature of electronic organs. With a harmonium, sound is produced immediately when a key is depressed and ceases immediately when a key is released. This significantly affects how you move your fingers on the keyboard and gives rise to many different playing styles. Which style you use depends greatly on the kind of music being played.

That said, this chapter focuses primarily on the use of the harmonium for personal or group devotional purposes, as befits this author's experience. Harmoniums can be and are used in various other musical styles, of course, and it's assumed that those readers who are so interested can adapt what's given here to their particular needs.

Also, while the sections below strive to describe how to play the harmonium in various ways, there really is no substitute for working directly with someone who has experience with the instrument. Words cannot fully describe how the hands move, nor can they give any indication about the sorts of sound that a harmonium can produce. So if you know someone who can help you, invite them over for dinner, engage them in good conversation about harmoniums (now you know why this book starts with a little history!), and find an appropriate moment to express your desire to learn to play. Chances are they'll be more than happy to share what they know with you.

Sitting at the Harmonium

One beautiful aspect of the Indian harmonium is that you can hold it or sit at it in any number of ways. You can place the harmonium on the floor and sit next to it in some cross-legged or straight-legged position (called "standard" position). You can also prop one end of it on one leg leaving the other end on the floor (called the "qawwali" position, after the traditional form of Islamic devotional music found in both India and Pakistan). If you prefer to sit in a chair, you can hold the harmonium in your lap, set it on another chair, or set it on a short table or footstool in front of you. And if you prefer to stand and stroll, it's a simple matter to attach a strap to the sides of the instrument with a couple of screws or pegs.[*]

Simply said, there is no "right" position—hold the instrument in whatever way you find comfortable. The same goes for which hand you use to pump the bellows and which one you use to play the keyboard. While most players pump with the left and play with the right, harmoniums easily accommodate the opposite position, especially those with top-fold bellows. In either case, it's helpful to keep your playing wrist straight, not bent or flexed, so that your playing fingers can remain as relaxed as possible.

Another helpful note is that some harmoniums sound brighter than others, sometimes to the point of being a little shrill. To tone down and soften the sound, lay a folded hand towel over the cover glass (or whatever else covers the back side of the keys). This both muffles the sound and makes a comfortable pad for your pumping hand.

---

[*] In a photographic book called *The World's Family* by Ken Heyman, there's a picture of a boy playing a harmonium that's hanging around his shoulders by a very thin cord. And if that isn't bad enough, he's also standing in the ocean!

Pumping the Bellows

An important part of getting a pleasant sound from a harmonium—especially as a solo instrument—is to maintain a fairly steady flow of air past the reeds. As mentioned in Chapter Two (pages 28–30), this is made possible by the internal bellows. Pulling in the external bellows "charges" the internal bellows through a one-way valve at a faster rate than the air can generally escape through open reeds. While the internal air discharges through the reeds, the external bellows can be let back out, to fill them with air again, and drawn back in without causing any interruption in the sound. So long as there is some air pressure within the internal bellows, you'll get a reasonably steady sound from the instrument as a whole.

As a simple first experiment, release the external bellows and allow them to open. Make sure at least one air stop is open. Now depress a key and firmly pull the external bellows back in and hold them there. You'll notice that as you hold the bellows in (or even allow them to fall back out again), the note continues to play for a few seconds.

As another experiment, fully pump the external bellows twice without holding any keys down. Now let go of the bellows and depress a key. The sound you hear is being entirely sustained by the internal bellows.

"Breathing": Producing a Steady Tone

Now repeat the first experiment, but *allow the external bellows to fall open* after drawing them in. Once those bellows have opened up, draw them immediately in again. Then let them *fall open*, draw them in, let them open, draw them in, and so on. In this way you can keep a note going as long as you like with a steady air flow.

When you have a good amount of air within the internal bellows, pumping the external bellows will feel a little stiffer or harder than when there's no internal air pressure. To get a feel for this, first drain all the air by holding down a few keys until there's no more sound. Now pump the external bellows a number of times without holding down any keys while paying close attention to how the bellows become increasingly stiff. Can you feel the pressure that's being built up? Now, pull in a little on the external bellows without collapsing them, and depress one or more keys. (Warning—the sound will probably be quite loud!) Can you feel the pressure fall off? Now pump the bellows again until they get a little stiff, hold down a key, and try to keep pumping the bellows such that you feel more or less the same stiffness all the time. You should get a fairly constant sound from the instrument as a result.

Notice how in these exercises you don't need to push the bellows open: as mentioned in Chapter Two, most harmoniums have some kind of spring that does this for you. (Some, however, do not, in which case you do need to push.) The practical effect of this is that once you've pulled the bellows in, you can just *open* your hand wide and allow the bellows to *fall into it*. This allows the bellows to refill with air as quickly as possible while leaving your hand ready to pull the bellows in again. The rate of air flow in and out of the external bellows is thus unequal: air comes in faster than it's pushed out (that is, into the internal bellows).

This is exactly how we breathe when we sing: a quick inhalation is followed by a long, steady exhalation, allowing us to sustain notes for a much longer time than it takes to inhale. When learning to play the harmonium, it is well worth the effort to pay attention to this method of "breathing" through the bellows until it becomes second nature. That steady air flow is everything.

Volume, Expression, and the Art of Pumping

Once you're comfortable sustaining a single note, you can begin to control the relative volume of that note. First *quicken* the speed at which you pull the bellows in (again, allowing the bellows to fall into your open hand). This will increase the volume. Now *slow* the speed at which you pull the bellows in. This will decrease the volume.

Now see just *how* slowly you can pump the bellows while still maintaining a soft, steady tone. The better the harmonium, the more softly you can sustain the sound. You may even hear one of the two reeds (usually the higher one) drop out. At this point, you can pump a little more quickly to re-engage that reed.

Just as the *speed* of pumping affects the volume, so does the *depth*. That is, by allowing the bellows to fall open more widely (or by pushing them more open) you'll move more air through the harmonium at any given rate of pumping, thereby increasing the volume. Conversely, if you allow the bellows to only open shallowly, you'll move less air and thus decrease the volume.

Quick, shallow pumping can thus produce the same volume as slow, deep pumping. At the same time, the dynamics of the two differ somewhat because of the corresponding response of the internal bellows. In effect, the movement of the internal bellows will generally mirror how you pump the external bellows. If your pumping is quick and shallow, the internal bellows will move quickly but shallowly. If your pumping is slow and deep, that's how the internal bellows will move as well.

Again, the steadiness of a harmonium's sound depends on the amount of air maintained in the internal bellows. If your pumping is quick and shallow, the same notes will not be sustained as long as if your pumping is slow and deep, even though they play at the same volume. This means that those notes might fall off somewhat more during those short intervals of time when the external bellows are being refilled with air. As a result, the harmonium sounds more "warbly" than steady (Figure 3-1).

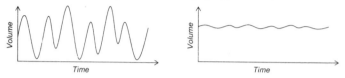

Figure 3-1 for the technically-minded: Warbling vs. steady sounds

A warbling sound is often the result of what we might call "timid" pumping. If you're actively playing on the keyboard, you can really pump the bellows quite vigorously without any fear of damaging them. Of course, there might be times when you really *want* a warbly sound rather than something more steady. It all depends on how you want to express the music that you're playing.

Where the bellows are concerned, expression on the harmonium comes from a combination of quick, slow, shallow, and deep pumping according to the feeling of the song. A *crescendo* is achieved by gradually increasing the speed and depth of the pumping action, while a *diminuendo* is achieved by gradually slowing down or pumping more shallowly. With a good instrument, you can also stop pumping altogether for a short time while you continue to play on the keyboard, thereby allowing the sound to gradually soften. The trick here, however, is to start pumping again a little *before* the volume diminishes to the point at which you want to sustain it. The same is true for accentuating specific notes or phrases; here you can give a quick, sudden pull to the bellows, then quickly resume your normal pumping rhythm.

With practice, again, these things can become a matter of feeling and intuition, whereby you no longer need to think about *how* you're pumping the bellows (fast, slow, shallow, and so forth). You can learn instead to *listen* to the sound and *feel* the bellows in your hand, making intuitive adjustments until you achieve the desired sound.

Repeat After Me: It's *Not* a Piano

In general, experience playing other keyboard instruments is helpful with playing the harmonium since the keyboard layout is the same. If you're unfamiliar with the keyboard, you'll probably find it helpful to label each key with bits of sticky notes, repeating, on a C-scale harmonium, C-D-E-F-G-A-B starting from the lowest note on the left side of the keyboard (see Figure 3-2).

Figure 3-2: How to label keys on a C-scale harmonium

When playing only a melody, one note at a time, the methods of fingering that one learns on a piano work fairly well on the harmonium. Such methods, however, can also be troublesome because they often rely on the piano's sustain capabilities. Again, a harmonium's sound cuts off almost immediately when you release a key. Playing a harmonium like a piano, then, will generally produce a pronounced *staccato* effect, and unless this is the intention (such as when you're playing as part of an ensemble) it can be rather distracting.

For this reason, most people, when playing solo harmonium, play with more *legato* (smoothness) to make the overall sound much more gentle and pleasant. *Legato* here means that you don't fully let up on a key until you've actually begun to depress another, while at the same time not necessarily playing the two notes simultaneously. This

51

might sound harder than it is; it's really just a matter of learning to move your fingers smoothly across the keys.

This can get complicated, however, if you are playing more than one note at a time (chords, for example). If you have to change the overall position of your hand from a set of low-range notes to a set of high-range notes (or vice versa), you effectively have to continuously hold a key down while changing *which* finger you're using to hold it down. This means that for brief periods of time you might be holding down one or more keys with more than one finger! This is certainly different from fingering methods for the piano.

What also differs a great deal from the piano is that you don't have to *strike* the keys to produce sound. In a piano, the keys are directly coupled to the movement of the hammers that strike the strings, so there is often a great deal of up-and-down movement in the wrist and quite a bit of tension in the fingers as is necessary to move the hammers against the strings.

With a harmonium, on the other hand, the keys only control the flow of air. This means you need almost no tension in the fingers, and the wrist can pretty much remain relaxed and level. Think of your playing hand as almost *floating* across the tops of the keys while your fingers simply *wiggle* enough to fully depress the keys. This is really all it takes! Indeed, if you strike the keys as you would on a piano, you'll actually make quite a bit of extraneous noise.*

In other words, to the extent that tension and force are necessary to play a piano, *relaxation and tenderness* are much the modus operandi of the harmonium, as befits it's devotional origins.

---

*It's much like the difference between an old manual typewriter, which requires a great deal of physical force to operate, and a computer keyboard, which takes very little.

Playing Styles: Introduction

Music plays upon our feelings and emotions perhaps more than any other form of communication. It can make us weep at a moment's notice; it can encourage us to risk our lives in battle; or it can inspire deep states of spiritual upliftment and devotion. It all depends on the consciousness expressed in any given song through its melody, harmony, and rhythm (including tempo) as well as through other factors such as lyrics.* Awareness of these factors enables us to use them most effectively with whatever instruments we play, especially with a devotional instrument such as the harmonium.

Melody—the relationship between successive notes—is the resonance of the heart's aspirations. A well-written melody takes us on a journey from wherever we are into some other state of consciousness, whether positive and negative. Upwardly soaring melodies literally lighten one's spirits, whereas a melody that never seems to get off the ground literally makes one feel heavy.

Harmonies—the relationship between *simultaneous* notes such as chords—express emotional depth. Harmonies awaken feeling in the heart—this much is certain. Yet those feelings may or may not assist the purpose of a song's melody. A light, soaring melody can be dragged down by too much emphasis on chords, especially heavy ones, or by harmonies that are simply "wrong" for the melody. Conversely, a rather gloomy melody can be brightened somewhat with lighter harmonies (but then why bother with gloomy melodies in the first place?).

Rhythm, finally, serves to ground a melody in the present (rather than allowing it to wax sentimentally about the

---

*Emotionally speaking, most people are generally affected more deeply by how a given piece of music *sounds* than by what its lyrics actually say. This is clearly seen in a great deal of popular music, in which the lyrics aren't even intelligible to begin with!

past or future) by emphasizing certain parts and de-emphasizing others. This too can have either a positive or a negative effect. Emphasis on the downbeat, for instance, makes music more emotional and, in some ways, more egoic. A rhythm that is sensitively attuned to the melody and lyrics, on the other hand, can effectively highlight the deeper or more inspiring parts, giving them a little more time to linger in the mind.

In this way, tempo is also an important consideration. Musical tempo is related in our subconscious to the heartbeat. For this reason, most songs and chants have a natural tempo or beat that is appropriate for both its melody and its lyrics. A light, joyful song naturally has a perkier pace that serves to awaken these same qualities in ourselves; a soothing, relaxing piece naturally moves more slowly, serving to induce calmness. It's simply self-defeating, then, to sing a joyful, energetic, or awakening melody with the kind of tempo that's appropriate for a lullaby, just as it is to sing a quiet, peaceful, inward song with a tempo designed to rouse one out of lethargy.

In addition, a hurried tempo makes it difficult to sing the words or to really feel the melody; a dragging tempo makes it difficult to follow the aspirations inherent in the melody and makes it more difficult to feel the meaning of the lyrics. In both cases, the words and the melody notes simply degenerate into nothing more than sounds, rather than being true expressions of the heart's feelings.

A good way to find the natural rhythm of a song—especially devotional chants—is to sing it *a capella*, that is, without any instrumental accompaniment, or to sing it only mentally. Better yet, simply *say* the words, out loud or mentally, at a pace you find meaningful, much as you would say a heartfelt (as opposed to a formal) prayer. Then say or "say-sing" the words on the melody, with that same tempo. Now that you've found a good tempo for the melody itself, you can work out a suitable accompaniment at this rhythm that truly serves the meaning and feeling of the song and doesn't distract from it. Otherwise, it's all too easy for the sound of the accompanying instrument itself to take center stage.

I say all this because the harmonium was, literally from its birth, designed for devotional rather than popular music—for the expression of spiritual consciousness, in other words, rather than for what is too often the mere production of noise. As we saw in Chapter One, harmoniums were mostly used in the West for singing hymns, at church and at home. In the East, harmoniums are to this day more often used for devotional music than anything else. Thus I encourage anyone learning to play the harmonium for such purposes to emphasize melody much more than harmony and to treat such music with the reverence and sensitivity of prayer. Good harmonies can certainly be helpful in strengthening the aspirations of the melody—awakening the heart's feelings, for instance, at the beginning of a devotional chant. But don't let harmonies keep things stuck on an emotional level: use them as a springboard, then forget about them and concentrate on infusing the melody and the lyrics with increasing power, depth, and meaning. Devotional singing and chanting can then become a powerful means for self-transformation, able to lift the mind from the doldrums of worldly existence into a meditative state of divine awareness.

Bearing all this in mind, the playing styles described in the following sections thus start and end with playing little more than a melody by itself. In the middle, we'll explore other stylistic variations that may help you to develop more depth or, shall we say, devotional efficacy in your playing. Indeed, you may, for a time, find great inspiration in one or the other style. Yet always remember to keep coming back to the melody, wherein the heart's aspirations are most purely expressed.

Single-Note Melody

One of the easier ways to begin playing the harmonium is simply to play a melody line by itself, one note at a time. It is also a very good method to use when playing in a group with other instruments (especially chord instruments such as guitars).

As described earlier, piano-style fingering (with a relaxed hand) can work fairly well here. Of course, this means either that you can read musical notation well enough or that you have a good enough ear to play songs without written music in front of you. If you boast neither skill but can learn the rhythm of the song, you can try writing out a song using just the words and the note that goes with each syllable. (This is where labeling the individual keys on the harmonium by their letter note is helpful.)

Here's an example, using Paramhansa Yogananda's popular chant, *Door of My Heart,* given first in musical notation, then written with note letters:

```
Gↆ Aↆ  C   D   D
Do-or of my heart,
    F  F   E    D C    D   Aↆ
    o-pen wide I keep for Thee (repeat)


F    F   F    E    E    D
Wilt Thou come? Wilt Thou come?,
    C   D   E D    C    D  Aↆ
    Just for o-once come to me. (repeat)


Gↆ  Aↆ  C   D   D D
Will my days fly away
    C   D   E D   C    D  Aↆ
    without seeing Thee, my Lord? (repeat)


F    F   F    E    E    D
Night and day, night and day,
    C D   E   D    C    D  Aↆ
    I look for Thee night and day. (repeat)
```

Here all the notes are relative to middle C; those notes marked with a down arrow (ↆ) are below middle C. You can also use an up arrow (↑) for notes that begin an octave above middle C.

In playing a melody by itself, make the transition between notes smooth to avoid a choppy sound. Depending on the song, this may take a little practice to find the best placement for the fingers at any given point in the melody. A little experience on the piano is again useful here. In the chant above, for instance, it's very helpful to play the first G note with the right index finger arching over the thumb so that the thumb can follow with the A. This leaves the whole hand in a good position to play the remaining melody notes, with the index finger on C, the middle finger on D, the ring finger on E, and the little finger on F.

The other helpful tip with this playing style is that *it is not necessary to play every note separately when successive notes are identical.* Playing notes separately means lifting your finger on that note, only to bring it down again, making the sound a little choppy. For a smoother, less distracting sound, hold the appropriate key down through successive syllables that use the same note. With this in mind, we can rewrite the chant above as follows:

```
G↓ A↓  C  D
Do-or of my heart,
        F     E    D C   D   A↓
        o-pen wide I keep for Thee (repeat)


F                E         D
Wilt Thou come? Wilt Thou come?,
        C    D  E D   C    D  A↓
        Just for o-once come to me. (repeat)


G↓  A↓  C    D
Will my days fly away
        C   D  E  D   C    D  A↓
        without seeing Thee, my Lord? (repeat)


F                E         D
Night and day, night and day,
        C D   E   D    C    D  A↓
        I look for Thee night and day. (repeat)
```

In other words, simply eliminate excess notes and let your singing voice accentuate the syllables. Indeed, the voice is really the primary instrument in any song (save instrumentals, of course)—through the words and the melody, the voice has the largest role in communicating the meaning or consciousness of the music. The harmonium then provides accompaniment and depth to the overall sound.

Now, if you are either less experienced at playing the harmonium or have a relatively weak voice (sans amplification), you might feel that the result of using this single-note melody style sounds rather "thin." This is not so much of an issue with personal singing or chanting; you should always use whatever you find most inspiring. When you're singing for a group, however, especially solo, there needs to be enough energy—in terms of sound and vibration—to invite everyone else's participation. Devotion—the heart's feelings directed upward toward God—necessitates there being *some* feeling in the heart to direct! Yogananda, in fact, suggested to first "whip up the feelings in the heart," after which they can be reined in and channeled upwards in the calmness of deep meditation.

If people can't hear you when they try to sing, chances are they won't sing at all. To involve others and to help awaken their heart's feelings, then, you can try playing with a "drone" note or employ other kinds of harmony elements as described in the next two sections. The challenge in both, of course, is how to gradually move away from a dependence on harmony and establish the melody as the means for taking a song inward. Such a playing style is described in the third section below. (If you're playing several songs in a row, you can try using drones and harmony more in earlier songs, gradually moving more toward melody in the later songs.)

Another helpful possibility with the single-note melody style is to employ the coupler (see Chapter Two, page 35) if available. Playing a single note on the keyboard will then sound four separate reeds in three octaves, producing a fuller tone.

Melody with Drone

To add some depth of feeling to a melody, many players I know, myself included, often use this style in personal and group settings. (Here one can also make effective use of rhythm *accidentals,* which are described in the last section on page 67.)

A *drone* is simply a note that's played continuously along with the melody. In some cases the drone note remains the same throughout the entire song. For example, the A below middle C works well as a drone for *Door of My Heart.* In this and any other cases, it also works to use one drone note for one part of a song, switch to a different drone note for another part, then switch back when the first part is repeated.

A small complication here is that the melody notes might overlap or fall adjacent to the drone note, as happens in *Door of My Heart*. When this occurs, you might want to temporarily let up on the drone to accentuate the note (when it's part of the melody, in which case you'd immediately depress it again) or simply avoid playing two adjacent notes (which can sound quite discordant).

In *Door of My Heart*, for instance, you can start playing on the low G by itself (no drone), then play the low A as befits the melody. You then hold the A (with the thumb) through the first line until you get to the last D. Then you can briefly let up on the A so that you can accentuate it in the melody. The same principle applies to the other lines, as shown below, where the top line indicates the drone ("x" meaning "no drone," "-" meaning continuous drone) and the middle line indicates the melody note as before:

```
X   A↓ - - -
G↓ A↓ C  D
Do-or of my heart,
         - - - - - - - - - x   A↓
         F   E   D C   D  A↓
         o-pen wide I keep for Thee (repeat)

A↓ - - - - - - - - - - - - -
F              E          D
Wilt Thou come? Wilt Thou come?,
       - - - - - - - - - - -x  A↓
       C   D  E D   C    D  A↓
       Just for o-once come to me. (repeat)

X    A↓ - - -
G↓   A↓ C    D
Will my days fly away
        - - - - - - - - - - -x  A↓
        C  D  E D   C     D  A↓
        without seeing Thee, my Lord? (repeat)

A↓ - - - - - - - - - - - - -
F             E          D
Night and day, night and day,
```

```
- - - - - - - - - - - x   A↓
C D   E   D   C   D   A↓
I look for Thee night and day. (repeat)
```

It can be something of an art to determine which drone notes are best for any given melody. Generally speaking, a middle C works well for songs in the key of C major. The A below middle C works well for songs in A major, D major, or A minor. The B below middle C works well for songs in G major or E minor. It's really a matter of experimentation or of asking a more experienced player, especially where switching drones is concerned. A good chant book such as *Wave of the Sea* (see page 70) also offers specific suggestions for drone notes.

As described in Chapter Two, most Indian harmoniums come with built-in drones that are activated by knobs on the front of the instrument. These particular drones are sometimes employed in various styles of Indian music and in some chanting. However, there are various reasons why many people seldom use these built-in drones:

- Built-in drones are usually notes such as $D^b/C^\#$, $E^b/D^\#$, $G^b/F^\#$, $A^b/G^\#$, and $B^b/A^\#$, and playing melodies in the necessary keys is generally more difficult than playing in keys such as C, D, and G.

- Built-in drones are softer than regular notes because they have only a single reed producing the sound. That reed, moreover, is usually thicker than others, so it doesn't vibrate as strongly. As a result, built-in drones usually fade out when other keys are played, thereby contributing less to the overall sound.

- It's difficult (though not impossible!) to change a built-in drone while you're playing.

Another option you have, as described in Chapter Two (see Figure 2-10, page 32) is to create any standing note you want by moving the key spring off that particular note.

To do this, lift off the cover glass and gently lift the curved spring on the back end of the appropriate key and move it to an adjacent key. The key will stay down until you move the spring back.

Now for the caveat: by playing a drone note together with melody notes, you are actually *creating harmonies.* These two-note chords aren't necessarily as full or rich—or, for that matter, emotional—as fuller three- or four-note chords, but they are chords nonetheless. And while the resulting sound may be perfectly suitable to the song in question, a drone can produce some inappropriate or decidedly unpleasant chords with certain melody notes. Play a middle C along with the B above it for a good example.*

If you run into problem spots like this, one solution is to simply stop playing the drone for a few notes and revert temporarily to the single-note style, bringing the drone back in when it's musically appropriate. Another way to get around this is to change the drone as often as needed to produce better intervals (that is, better harmonies) between the drone note and the melody note. But before exploring this style in detail, it's good to know a little more about chords themselves.

Chords

Some people who are first learning to play the harmonium, including children I've worked with, find it easier (and more gratifying) to start first by playing chords before learning to play (and emphasize) melodies. This is because the chords in a song generally change much less frequently than melody notes. In addition, many songs can be played with a combination of only two or three chords that are relatively easy to switch between.

---

*Which is not to say that such a combination is never used in music; it's actually part of a "C major 7th" chord. Such a chord, however, must be used sensitively. On a harmonium it often sounds disconcerting if held for more than a passing beat.

For example, one of the simplest "starter chants" for playing chords is a rendition of Yogananda's *Listen, Listen, Listen.* Once you memorize the rhythm to such a chant, it's helpful (as with the melody shown on page 57) to write out the chords above the lyrics:

```
G                              Em
Listen, listen, listen to my heart song (repeat)

   G                              Em
I will never forget Thee, I will never forsake Thee
(repeat)
```

Since it involves only two chords, G and E minor (as shown in Figures 3-3a and 3-3b), new harmonium players can get the feeling of the bellows and the keys without too many other complications. (Both books listed at the end of this chapter, page 70, contain the melody to this song.)

Figures 3-3a, 3-3b: G (top) and E minor (bottom) chords

To play these chords as shown, and assuming you're playing with the right hand, place your thumb on the B (the lowest key), the index finger on the D (middle key in Figure 3-3a), the middle finger on the E (middle key in Figure 3-3b), and the little finger on the G (the highest key). Switching between the two chords is then simply a matter of alternating between the index (D) and middle (E) fingers while keeping the thumb and little finger in place.

Realistically speaking, though, most songs involve at least three chords, some as many as six or more, making them obviously more complicated to play in this style. Yet many different pairs of chords (major or minor) share at least one note between them. C and F chords, for instance, which are commonly used with the G chord, share the C note; C and G chords share the G note. Similarly, A, D, and G chords are often used together; A and D chords share the A note while D and G chords share the D note.

This means that when you change between such chords you can hold down whichever finger is on the shared note while changing the other notes with your other fingers. This way you'll maintain a smooth, continuous sound.

In some chord transitions you won't have any notes in common: F and G, for instance, or G and A. Here you have to change every note to some other note while avoiding distracting moments during which the harmonium's sound is cut out completely. Otherwise you end up with something that can only be described as BLAAAT <silence> BLOOOT <silence> BLEEET <silence> BLAAAT, and so on. This isn't something I recommend very highly.

Practice helps you make chord changes sound good: the less you have to move your playing hand to change chords, the easier and smoother the resulting sound will be. You can also help yourself out tremendously by carefully choosing which chord "inversions" you actually play. For more details on this subject, see Appendix B, page 129.

As a practical note, it's not necessary to practice smooth transitions between *every* possible combination of chords. Most songs and chants involve only a handful of chords, and those often occur together as a group. If you only learn, for instance, to smoothly transition between C, F, and G chords, you'll be able to play many songs written in the key of C.

The following table shows other common trios of major and minor chords according to key. I encourage you, especially when learning a new piece, to play around with different combinations of inversions in each group and find a combination that works well for your playing hand.

Major Key	Major Chords	Minor Key	Minor Chords
C	C, F, G	Am	Am, Dm, Em
D	D, G, A	Bm	Bm, Em, F#m
G	G, C, D	Em	Em, Am, Bm
A	A, D, E	F#m	F#m, Bm, C#m

Note that the major and minor chords shown in the same row of the table often show up together in the same song (as in *Listen, Listen, Listen*). If you're feeling comfortable with your ability to transition between the individual major or minor trios, you can also practice mixing up the major and minor chords as well, again finding combinations of inversions that work for you. *Door of My Heart,* as an example, is a great one to practice most of the chords in the C and Am groups:

```
C        Dm G
Door of my heart,
     F                      Am
     open wide I keep for Thee (repeat)


F          Dm    Am        Dm
Wilt Thou Come? Wilt Thou come?
     F                      Am
     Just for once come to me. (repeat)


C            Dm
Will my days fly a-way
     F                      Am
     without seeing Thee, my Lord? (repeat)


F          Dm    Am        Dm
Night and day, night and day,
     F                      Am
     I look for Thee night and day. (repeat)
```

One last point on making smooth transitions between chords: *it's not necessary to depress all the notes for the new chord simultaneously.* It might be easier in various circumstances to switch to two notes of the new chord first, then bring in the third note a few moments later. This might make it easier in turn for you to learn to play certain transitions, as you'll only need to remember two note changes instead of three. In many cases you might elect to simply stick with a two-note chord instead of a fuller one.

The situations in which this is helpful depends on the chords in question and whether the sound produced even fits the song—separating the notes can easily become distracting if used insensitively. In any case, it's important to understand that there is no rule that says you *have* to press every note in the new chord at once. After all, the real goal is to produce an accompaniment that is pleasant to the ear, warming to the heart, and uplifting to the spirit. You're always free to do whatever draws you closer to that goal.

Melody with Chord-Appropriate Drones

In this style the drone note is changed as often as necessary to bring chords and the melody together. This is especially useful when playing along with a chord instrument, such as a strummed guitar, wherein the harmonium may need to both carry the melody *and* match the guitar chords. Playing a single-note melody in such situations works quite well, of course, but if you want to have the harmonium more fully in the picture *you will need to change drones as appropriate to the chord being played on the guitar.*

When you're playing solo harmonium, this style is also quite effective at avoiding oddball intervals between drone and melody notes. At the same time, it isn't always the best choice because there can often be too many drone/ chord changes to allow one to become inwardly focused.

In playing solo harmonium, then, you might want to stick to single-note melody or use drones in such a way as to fall somewhere between this style and playing the same drone throughout. That strikes a pretty good balance. The other option is to refine your playing style even further, which is discussed in the next section.

The whole idea with this style is that the highest note being played is almost always the melody note, and that any other notes being played are both appropriate to the mode of the song and to the chords being used.

This is obviously a more complicated technique, and it might take some time to learn it because of the demands it makes on your fingers. It's also more difficult to write out musical notation for this sort of thing—essentially you end up writing exactly which notes should be played when. In the end, it's really a technique to try when you're both fairly fluent with a melody and familiar enough with chords to effectively make drone decisions on the fly.

There are still times when no drone works and you just have to forget the drone for a few melody notes and pick it up later. I've experienced this playing with a friend who sometimes uses what he calls "Led Zeppelin" chords on his twelve-string guitar that I can't even identify (like an F# augmented 4th minor somesuch seventh). All I can really do in cases like this is just stick to the melody and wait for some chord that I can decipher!

Melody with Semi-Chorded Drones and Rhythm Accidentals

Befitting the long-winded title that I've given it, this style is definitely the most advanced, incorporating elements of most of the other styles. Here we:

a. Incorporate chords or drones *at times*, to make the sound richer when the feeling of the chant seems to *want* a richer sound

b. Lay off the drones entirely when the feeling is more purely expressed through the melody, while we also

c. Bring in *momentary* drone or chord elements both to accentuate the rhythm of the song and to maintain an appropriately "full" sound. (By itself, this is quite useful when playing the melody with drone style as well.)

Suffice it to say that this style is really one to express personal inspiration and intuition rather than some predefined stylistic form. It's also a style that really has to be observed to appreciate; words don't do it justice.

That said, using drones here doesn't always make the same chord interval that would be appropriate if you were playing with a guitarist. The intervals might also sound "bad" in and of themselves but either are held for such a short duration that they go unnoticed or become an integral part of the overall feeling of the song or chant. In addition, the drone might actually be the *highest* note you're playing, rather than the lowest—that is, you might be playing a few melody notes below the note being held as the drone.

This is especially true when one also uses *accidentals* to accentuate the rhythm. Accidentals are brief tappings on one or more notes that are generally part of the appropriate chord for whatever point you happen to be in the melody. Sometimes these notes can also be dragged—held a little longer—to add a little extra strength to a phrase. However, because accidentals are generally so short, they don't necessarily *have* to be part of such a chord. You might sometimes use accidentals composed of two notes that are side by side, such as an A and a B or a G and an A. If these were played for any noticeable length of time they'd sound awful, but when tapped only momentarily they produce an effect more like that of a drum.* This effect can help one keep a good rhythm along with the lyrics when the melody note remains the same across several beats. It also helps keep the rhythm when singing a chant *mentally,* without making it necessary to play every individual melody note.

To give you an idea of what this looks like, Figure 3-4 on page 71 shows a hopefully reasonable representation of my rendition of Yogananda's chant, *I Will Sing Thy Name,* where the highest note is always the melody. As you can see, there's quite a lot happening elsewhere on the keyboard!

With this playing style, you can begin a song or chant (especially a repetitive one) by energetically playing the melody along with full chords to really awaken the heart's feelings. As the chant is repeated and turns a little softer, you can begin to drop notes out of various chords, thereby thinning the harmonium's sound a little and allowing the heart's feelings to turn a little more inward. As the chant becomes softer and more inward still, you can more and more release all notes except those in the melody until you reach the point where you're primarily playing the melody with only occasional accidentals, if any, to keep the rhythm. In the space of one chant, then, you can transition from a full, outward sound to a very inward sound, without losing any energy along the way.

As I said, words can hardly do this sort of thing justice, especially considering that how far and how quickly you actually depress a key do have certain subtle effects on the resulting sound (but not as they have on a piano). Truly, to really learn this technique will require the guidance and example of a skilled harmonium player and a great deal of practice.

---

*Swami Gyanananda, a Swiss man who journeyed to India many years ago to become a monk (see *Shaped by Saints,* by Devi Mukerjee, Crystal Clarity Publishers), even uses the bellows of his harmonium as a drum, slapping it with his pumping hand between pumps.

Sources of Chant Music

There are two main sources of printed chant music generally composed for use with an Indian harmonium.

Cosmic Chants, by Paramhansa Yogananda (Self-Realization Fellowship, Los Angeles, California), contains the gamut of Yogananda's compositions in standard melody notation.

Wave of the Sea (Crystal Clarity Publishers, Nevada City, California) was put together by experienced harmonium players. It includes the melodies of many of Yogananda's most popular chants as well as many written by his disciple, Swami Kriyananda (J. Donald Walters). It includes melodies in musical notation with, letter notes, suggested drone notes, and suggested chords for both harmonium and guitar. An excellent book for all levels.

You can hear these chants performed on a number of recordings:

On *Music for Meditation* (Crystal Clarity), Swami Kriyananda plays many of Yogananda's chants in a way suitable for public performance (that is, predictable tempo and repetition).

On *Kriyananda Chants Yogananda* (Crystal Clarity), he plays chants in a more personal, devotional manner.

Chants & Prayers and *Songs of My Heart* (Self-Realization Fellowship) are recordings of Yogananda chanting himself.

Crystal Clarity offers other recordings such as *Wave of the Sea* that include many of the same chants as well as traditional Indian *bhajans.* Self-Realization Fellowship also offers additional recordings, and as the Indian genre is becoming increasingly popular, you can find many more at stores carrying "world music."

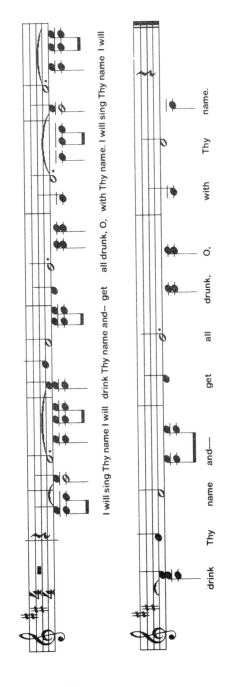

Figure 3-4: The author's (sideways) rendition of *I Will Sing Thy Name* with Semi-Chorded Drones and Rhythm Accidentals. The notes with ascending stems are the melody. The notes with descending stems are the accidentals, played with more *staccato*. Musically trained readers will appreciate the difficulty of notation here; rests have not been indicated between the accidentals.

—CHAPTER FOUR—

The Inner Realms

The inner workings of a hand harmonium are fairly simple and yet quite fascinating. It's fun to see how such a simple device can produce such beautiful music.

This chapter is primarily an exploration of the harmonium's inner anatomy, which sets the stage for Chapter Five, "Adjustments, Corrections, and Tuning." The various procedures detailed in Chapter Five will make reference to sections of this chapter for accessing different areas within the instrument.

In exploring these areas, you'll gain a deeper understanding of how the instrument actually does what it does. While all this isn't essential knowledge for playing and enjoying the instrument, various technically minded readers will no doubt benefit from this understanding. If, on the other hand, you are not of a mechanical temperament, you may safely ignore this and the following chapter unless you wake up one morning with an insatiable urge to tinker.

Indian harmoniums have four general anatomical areas, which we'll literally "get into" through the course of this chapter:

A. The external areas, such as the bellows, knobs, and faceplates

B. The keyboard and air holes above the reeds

C. The inner reed chamber, where the reeds and the air stops live

D. The lower bellows chamber

At the end of this chapter, we'll also see how the two bellows work together, as promised in Chapter Two.

GENERAL CAUTION:
Most Indian harmoniums are primarily constructed with a soft fir wood, both inside and out. Other harmoniums use a higher-quality wood such as teak on the outside but still use the soft fir on the inside. Be very careful, then, to not over-tighten screws when replacing them lest you strip the screw hole. If you do strip a hole, you may need to replace the screw with a slightly larger one. The other option is to fill the hole with putty or glue, wait for it to dry, then drill a small pilot hole for the original screw.

A. External Areas

Since the bellows, knobs, and faceplates are already on the outside of the instrument (Figure 4-1), there's obviously nothing tricky about getting to them! But there are a few concerns with these parts.

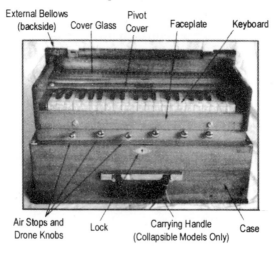

Figure 4-1: Harmonium externals

FACEPLATE SPACING

For proper operation of the keyboard, there should always be a little gap between it and the faceplate (Figure 4-2a). If the faceplate is on too tightly (Figure 4-2b), its inner edge will rub against the keys and cause them to get stuck

Figures 4-2a, 4-2b: Proper (left) and improper (right) faceplate gaps

in the down position. (This usually happens in the middle of the faceplate more than the ends.) The obvious solution is to back the faceplate screws out slightly. However, you may find that after doing so the faceplate is no longer tight against the main body of the harmonium. To solve this problem, remove the faceplate and locate the one or two spacer screws—or nails—if they exist (Figure 4-3); there

Figure 4-3: Faceplate spacers

may be one in the middle or one on each side, or both. Back these screws out a little bit (a half-turn or so, or pull a bit on the nails) so that the faceplate can be screwed down tightly without making contact with the keys. If, on the other hand, your harmonium doesn't have any such spacer screws, you can simply add one in the middle which should be sufficient.

Adjusting and Removing the Knobs

I mentioned in Chapter Two that you don't want to rotate the knobs too much, lest you either detach the knob from whatever it's connected to inside or cause that inner mechanism to be partially activated even when the knob is fully pushed in.

When you pull a knob out, you'll see that it's connected to a slender shaft. Each shaft goes some distance into the harmonium, where it connects to a block of wood: This block serves either as an air stop or as a base on which a drone reed or the tremolo is mounted (visible in Figure 2-11, page 33).

Each shaft is threaded on the end and screwed into its corresponding block of wood. Thus, if you rotate a knob clockwise, you effectively shorten the overall length of the shaft. If you do this too much, the shaft becomes too short for the block to return to its full "in" position (Figure 4-4). Remember this when removing and reinstalling the knobs.

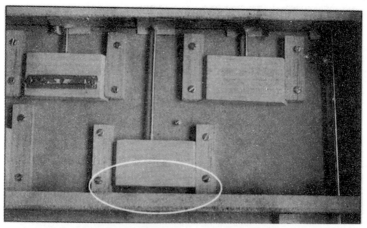

Figure 4-4: Air stop partially open due to over-tightening of knob and shaft (middle) and in the correct position (top right). A long shaft with two seals is visible on the right side.

If you twist counter-clockwise, you will eventually disconnect the shaft from the block. This is necessary, of course, if you intend to remove the knob and shaft altogether (necessary to access the inner bellows).

However, once the shaft is loose, don't just pull it straight out of the instrument. Rather, pull it only until you feel some resistance; this is where the threaded end meets an internal leather seal (visible along the top of Figure 4-4). At this point, spin the shaft counter-clockwise to gently thread it through the leather. This ensures that the leather seal remains as tight as possible.

Note that the longer shafts (usually for the male reeds) typically go through *two* seals (visible on the right side of Figure 4-4), so you'll need to be doubly careful.

If you're removing all the knobs, it's a good idea to lay them out in the order they were removed or, better yet, label them. Also, be careful to thread the shafts clockwise through the leather seals when reinserting the knobs, and be careful not to over-tighten them into the wooden blocks.

THE EXTERNAL BELLOWS

An important aspect of the external bellows is the specific spring mechanism that causes them to open automatically when the latch is released. On top-fold bellows, this "spring" is nothing more than a little rod bent 90 degrees at both ends, with the direction of the bends also offset by 90 degrees (Figure 4-5). When the rod is installed, it's *twisted* so that the two ends are pointing in the same direction. One end is then attached to the case while the other end sticks up into the back plate of the bellows (Figure 4-6). In this state, the rod naturally wants to return to its 90-degree offset position; thus, when the bellows latch is released, the torsion in the rod pulls the bellows open.

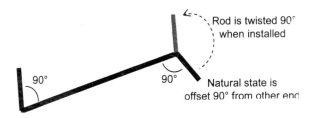

Figure 4-5: Design of a torsion spring rod in a top-fold bellows harmonium

Figure 4-6: A torsion spring rod as installed

On side-fold models, there is actually a spiral spring mounted *inside* the bellows.[*] You can see this by removing the screws that hold the valve (Figure 4-7) on the back of the bellows and gently prying the valve off if necessary. The spring is generally located to the left of the valve (looking at the back of the instrument) and is held in place with a small screw or two (Figure 4-8).

Figure 4-7: Rear bellows valve

Figure 4-8: The spiral spring inside side-fold bellows

[*]This is at least true of Bina models; harmoniums from some manufacturers (such as Dwarkin & Sons) don't have these internal springs.

B. Keyboard and Key Mechanisms

To get into the whole keyboard mechanism, follow these steps:

1. Remove the cover glass (or wood) by pulling on the small tab in the center of the cover. If this tab is missing, simply pry the cover up with a screwdriver or grab it in whatever other way seems convenient. Be gentle here so you don't damage the wood.

2. Remove the pivot cover (the piece of trim that goes across all the keys) by removing the screws on both ends (see Figure 2-19, page 40). Note that this piece is more than just trim: it also prevents the keys from popping off their pivot pins! Note: if you are working on a standard harmonium and will also need to access the reed chamber, follow step 2 under section C (page 83) instead to save yourself a little trouble.

You now have access to the entire keyboard mechanism, where you can make various adjustments. Figure 4-9 shows the different elements of the keyboard mechanism; Figure 4-10 highlights specific parts of the key.

You can see in Figure 4-9 that each key extends all the way to the back of the instrument; these are the ends you see moving under the cover glass when playing the instrument. The most common design (as found in the Bina models) is called a *pallet key* (Figures 4-11a and 4-11b). Here the holes that allow air to flow past the reeds for a particular note are covered by the end of the key itself; bits of leather attached to the key form a seal when the key is down. The pallet key pivots on a small vertical *pivot pin* located underneath the pivot cover. A simple wire key spring pushes a key back to its rest position when released.

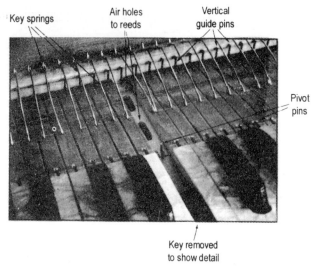

Key springs

Air holes to reeds

Vertical guide pins

Pivot pins

Key removed to show detail

Figure 4-9: Elements of a harmonium keyboard

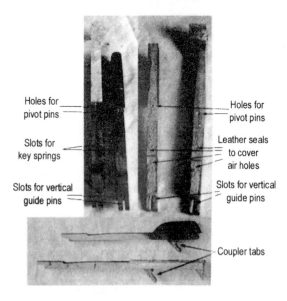

Holes for pivot pins

Holes for pivot pins

Slots for key springs

Leather seals to cover air holes

Slots for vertical guide pins

Slots for vertical guide pins

Coupler tabs

Figure 4-10: Elements of harmonium keys from top (left) and bottom (right).
Keys for use with a coupler have additional tabs on the bottom.

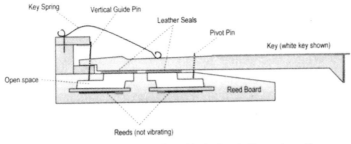

Figure 4-11a: A pallet key design with the key in the rest position

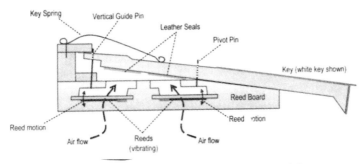

Figure 4-11b: A pallet key design with the key pressed down

The key's up and down motion is restricted by a horizontal wooden slat that holds all the key springs. A vertical guide pin, the corresponding slot on the end of the key, and the stiffness of the pivot pin all restrict the key's side-to-side motion. Nevertheless, every pallet key will move a little from side to side; if you happen to push or pull a key too hard to one side while the adjacent key is depressed, you may find that the first key doesn't pop up when you release it because of the friction on the sides (Figure 4-12). Normally this isn't a problem—if, however, you discover it to be so, first see if you can play with less sideways force on the keys. If that

Figure 4-12: A sticky key due to sideways friction

81

doesn't seem to be the issue, adjustments can be made to restrict the key's motion. (See "Sticky Keys" in Chapter Five, page 110.)

While the pallet design is quite common, there are other ways to restrict a key's sideways motion. In a lifting key design (such as that used by the Calcutta manufacturer Dwarkin & Sons, Figure 4-13), each key has a small metal pivot pin running through it horizontally (visible in the middle of the keys that are removed). Each key sits in a slot that is cut into a piece of wood that runs the width of the keyboard (center of picture); a tiny slot for the pivot pin runs crosswise to the key slot. These two slots restrict the side-to-side motion of the key, so no additional guide is necessary. When a key is depressed, its tail end lifts up on a shorter hinged piece of wood from which hangs a small block that seals the air holes. This block is heavy enough to return a key to the upright position when released. There are also small screws at the end of each key to adjust the exact placement of its upright position.

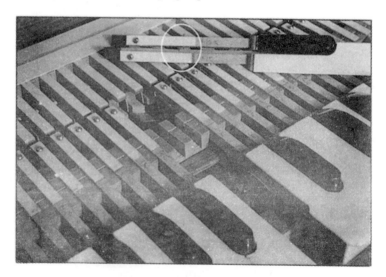

Figure 4-13: A lifting key design

C. Reed Chamber

To access the inner reed chamber, follow these steps:

1. Remove the cover glass (or wood; see step 1 under section B, page 79).

2. If you have a standard (that is, non-collapsible) harmonium, remove—as one piece—the pivot cover *and* the two side blocks by removing the screws that hold the side blocks to the main body of the harmonium (Figure 4-14). After you have removed these two screws, the pivot cover and the side blocks will come out as one piece. This is necessary on fixed-model harmoniums because the metal L-brackets on the backside typically prevent you from flipping up the keyboard assembly with the side blocks in place. You could, of course, remove the L-brackets instead—but besides there being more screws to deal with in the bracket, the hinge latches used with side-fold bellows go through these brackets, making them all the more difficult to remove. So it's easiest to just take out the pivot cover and side blocks together.

Figure 4-14: Removing the side blocks and pivot cover together

3. Remove the front faceplate (see Figure 4-1, page 74) by removing the two screws that hold it in place. After you've removed this piece you'll see hinges on which the entire keyboard assembly pivots and possibly those that are part of the coupler (Figure 4-15). (But don't remove any of the hinges for this procedure.)[*]

4. Locate and remove the two large screws at the back of the keyboard assembly (Figure 4-16).

Figure 4-15 (above): The upper hinges work with the coupler; the lower hinges are attached to the keyboard assembly.

· Figure 4-16 (above): Rear keyboard assembly screw (one on each side)

Figure 4-17 (right): The keyboard assembly flips up to expose the reed chamber

[*]Some models from manufacturers other than Bina have hinges on the outside, and no faceplate. They also have two latching handles rather than the screws in step 4.

At this point the entire keyboard will swing up from the backside (Figure 4-17), giving you access to the reed chamber and all the stops and drones (Figure 4-18). The reeds themselves are attached on the backside of the keyboard assembly.

To reinstall the keyboard assembly, simply perform the steps above in reverse order. Note that the rear screws should be tightened down firmly, as this is "instrumental" in maintaining good inner air pressure. Again, be careful not to over-tighten the faceplate, as indicated earlier.

Finally, you may find that the cover glass no longer fits after you replace the pivot cover. If this happens, slightly loosen the screws either on the pivot cover itself or on the side blocks so that the pivot cover can move a little toward

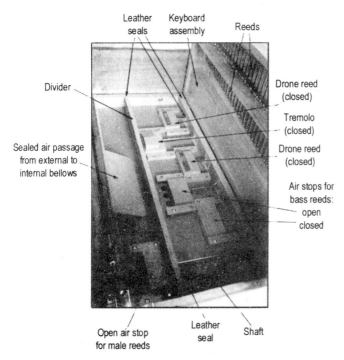

Figure 4-18: The reed chamber of a six-knobbed Bina Model 23B collapsible harmonium, where the reeds, stops, and drones are accessible

85

the front of the instrument. When you find a position that allows the cover glass to sit snugly, tighten the screws down fully. The same applies if there's too much of a gap between the cover glass and the pivot cover, in which case you can move the pivot cover toward the back a bit.

A Little Inside Tour

Now that we're inside the reed chamber, let's have a look around. Again, all of the reeds are attached to the underside of the keyboard assembly itself. If you look carefully (but not that carefully), you'll see that one set of reeds is larger than the other: this is the bass set; the smaller is the male set. If you have a third set of reeds that's even smaller, that's a female set.

Looking at Figure 4-18, you'll see a piece of white leather attached at a slant. This is where air from the external bellows is directed into the internal bellows. This piece of leather must be completely sealed if the bellows are to operate optimally. If you have a "wheezer" harmonium, this is a good place to look. You'll also see narrow strips of leather attached all around the perimeter of the reed chamber where the keyboard assembly makes contact. These too must create good seals if the harmonium is to maintain good internal air pressure.

You'll also notice that the "stop board" as I call it—the flat board to which all the air stops and such are attached—is divided into two chambers. The divider has leather seals on the top to isolate the two chambers.

In the particular harmonium shown, the chamber on the left has only a single air stop with three holes that open into the internal bellows. This stop opens air flow to the reeds on the rear of the keyboard assembly, typically the male set (which needs less air to operate than bass reeds). In the right chamber, we see (going from bottom to top), two air stops for the other set of reeds (typically the bass set), a drone reed, the tremolo, and a second drone reed.

You can also see the shafts that connect the external knobs to each little block of wood that forms either an air stop, a drone, or the tremolo. Notice where the shafts penetrate the sidewall of the reed chamber: at each point you'll see another little piece of leather that prevents all but a little air from leaking through these holes. You can also see a second seal on the side of the divider where the male air stop goes through.

This is why you don't want to just yank a knob and shaft out once it's been detached from its block, lest you tear the leather with the threads on the end of the shaft. Again, it's better to gently pull the shaft out until the threads meet the leather, then spin the shaft counterclockwise to thread the end through the leather.

With the whole reed chamber visible, you can easily see which knobs are attached to which air stops, which knobs control drone notes, and which knob (if any) is attached to the tremolo. You might want to jot down what you discover here for later reference. And if you look carefully at the drone reeds themselves, you should also see little markings such as *Cx* or *Gx* which indicate the exact note ("x" means sharp). You will probably want to note these as well.

Removing and Cleaning Reeds

While we're inside the reed chamber, it's a good time to discuss removing and cleaning reeds as mentioned in Chapter Two.

On the underside of the keyboard, each reed is held in place with two small slot-head screws (Figure 4-19). One of these goes through a hole in the reed frame; the other goes through a slot.

You do not need to remove both screws—you need only to *loosen* the one in the slot by a half-turn to a turn. The reeds are designed this way to make them easier to

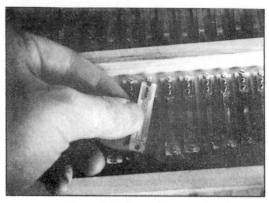

Figure 4-19: Removing a reed

remove and reinsert: the screw in the slot can hold the reed in place while you replace the screw through the hole.

You may find that the reeds seem glued in place; sometimes it's only that the person who made the instrument didn't wait for the varnish on the wood to dry before installing the reeds! Whatever the case, you can use a small flathead screwdriver to gently pry the reed out. *Gently* is an important concept here—you don't want to use so much force on the reed frame that you permanently bend it. Practically speaking, you may need to pry a little bit around different parts of the frame before the whole thing comes loose.

Dirt and other deposits can accumulate on either side of a reed. To give any one reed a good and thorough cleaning, it's best to remove it and work over both sides. Any cleaner that is suitable for brass is suitable for reeds, and you can certainly use nylon or plastic brushes if desired. Steel wool and other metallic abrasives are not recommended, of course, as you may inadvertently remove material from the reed and possibly change its tuning.

If you're removing all the reeds at once for whatever reason, it certainly makes sense to set them all out in order. Of course, since each reed is marked and since the different octaves are of different sizes, it's not impossible to sort them out again if your cat happens to take a leisurely feline stroll across your worktable or something like that. In any case, you at least don't need to worry about the screws—they're all interchangeable.

D. Lower Bellows Chamber

To access the lower bellows chamber and to remove the entire stop/drone board, first follow all the instructions for accessing the reed chamber. Then:

1. Carefully remove all the knobs as described earlier. Set these aside in the order they come out, or label them, so you can replace them correctly. (Nevertheless, it's not too hard to determine which length of shaft will fit which stop.)

2. Detach the keyboard assembly from its pivot hinges (visible in Figure 4-15, page 84). NOTE: If your harmonium is equipped with a coupler, detach the *lower* (larger) set of hinges; the upper (smaller) hinges are part of the coupler mechanism. Also, you need to remove only the upper screws; there is no need to remove the whole hinge. **Be careful not to drop the tiny screws down into the lower bellows chamber!** Trust

me on this one: they can be very difficult to fish out, especially if you're in the process of putting everything back together. Anyway, once you detach the hinges, the whole assembly will lift out (Figure 4-20).

Figure 4-20: Removing the keyboard

3. Remove the four screws that hold the "stop board" to the main body (Figure 4-21). This board will then lift out with the lower bellows (Figure 4-22).

Figure 4-21: Two screws (arrows) on each side of the stop board (four total) hold the stop board to the case.

Figure 4-22: Lifting out the stop board with the internal bellows

Figure 4-23: A lower bellows spring

4. This exposes the internal springs that push up the internal bellows (Figure 4-23). The springs might be attached to the bottom of the bellows (as in Figure 4-23) and might also be screwed to the bottom of the case. To remove these screws, you'll have to carefully reach in past the internal bellows to remove these screws.

Congratulations! You have now completely dismantled a harmonium! To reassemble the instrument, simply reverse the procedure. One important caution, though: before you screw the stop board back to the case (reversing step 3), *be sure that the loose ends of the hinges are up* (Figure 4-24a) *rather than wedged between the stop board and the case* (Figure 4-24b). Trust me on this one too!

Figure 4-24a: Proper hinge   Figure 4-24b: Don't do this!

The Inner Workings of the Bellows

As described briefly in Chapter Two, the two bellows work in tandem through two one-way valves. These devices are really nothing more than a set of holes with an unglamorous flap of leather attached to one side (typically the top), but they effectively allow air to flow in one direction but not the other.

When the external bellows drop away from the harmonium (aided by the spring or the torsion rod), the rear valve on the outside of the bellows opens to allow air to flow in while the second valve, located between the external and internal bellows, closes to prevent any air pressure within the internal bellows from escaping (Figure 4-25).

When the external bellows are drawn in, the rear valve closes to prevent air from escaping. Pressure builds in the

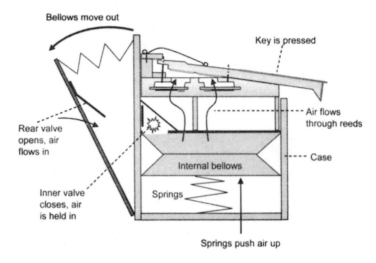

Figure 4-25: The internal valve closes when the external bellows move out

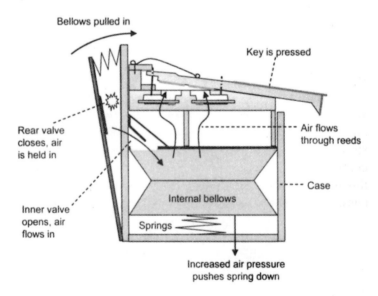

Figure 4-26: The rear valve closes when the external bellows move in

external bellows, causing the internal valve to open, thus charging the internal bellows against the internal springs (Figure 4-26).

If one or more keys are depressed, the compressed air within the internal bellows is allowed to flow past the appropriate reeds, resulting in sound. This sound will continue as long as air pressure remains within the internal bellows, regardless of what's happening with the external bellows; the internal springs provide this pressure automatically.

This two-bellows design is what makes a continuous air flow possible. The first pulling-in of the external bellows will charge the internal bellows with air at a faster rate, generally speaking, than the air can escape through open reeds (even if many keys are depressed at once). When the external bellows are let back out again, there is still enough pressure in the internal bellows to maintain a flow of air which, in turn, maintains a more-or-less steady sound.

Every harmonium varies in terms of how long the internal bellows can sustain a good air flow, depending on the stiffness of the internal bellows and the strength of the springs. The springs should be strong enough to push all the air out of the internal bellows. If they're too weak, you won't get a good air flow, even when the internal bellows are filled with air. On the other hand, if the springs are too strong, they won't ever allow the internal bellows to fill completely, thus also limiting the air flow. Fortunately, this is one of many problems that can be corrected, as discussed in the next chapter.

CHAPTER FIVE

Adjustments, Corrections, and Tuning

If you observe the few simple guidelines described toward the end of Chapter Two, an Indian harmonium will serve you well for many years. Nevertheless, most instruments, from time to time, develop one or more common problems, usually resulting from changes in temperature, humidity, dust, lint, the rigors of transportation, or simply age. Most problems are minor and are fairly simple to correct. Other adjustments are more intricate, and although the procedures are described here, you might elect to leave them in the hands of someone who has worked with harmonium internals before.

Each section of this chapter describes certain symptoms of a "malfunctioning" harmonium, the possible causes, how to determine the specific cause, and what to do about it. The coverage here is meant to be extensive, but not necessarily exhaustive. In addition, don't fear that your harmonium will develop all or even *any* of these conditions. Many instruments operate without trouble for years on end. But in case you encounter one of these symptoms, have hope! There is always a solution.*

- **Buzzing or rattling noises:** caused by loose cover glass, a misaligned reed, a sunken pivot pin, or foreign material inside the harmonium

- **Rumbling noises:** caused by loose trim or the lock

- **Squeaking noises:** caused by rubbing of a key's guide slot against the vertical guide pin, rubbing

---

*Although the coupler mechanism is occasionally involved with other issues, working with the coupler itself isn't covered in this edition.

of the pivot latch on side-fold bellows, or rubbing of the bellows spring on top-fold bellows

- **Ticking noises:** caused by key springs bumping into the cover glass, the mechanics of a coupler, rubbing of the pivot latch on side-fold bellows, or a maladjusted spring inside side-fold bellows

- **Leaky keys:** caused by old or misaligned leather seals or by misalignment of the pivot pin

- **Sticky keys:** caused by the face plate being on too tight, bent vertical guide pins, or misaligned leather seals

- **Loose or wobbly keys:** caused by a loose pivot pin, a split in the reed board, a sunken pivot pin, or a loose pivot cover

- **"Wheezing,"** lack of sustain, or an overall weak sound: caused by leaky inner leather seals or leaky bellows, a curled rear bellows valve, stiff inner bellows, or inner springs that are either too weak or too strong

- **Slow, fast, or non-sounding notes:** caused by maladjustment of a reed's position in its frame or by foreign matter that prevents the reed from vibrating

- **Out-of-tune notes:** caused by dirt, aging, or manufacturing defects

The procedures given in this chapter rely on the steps listed in Chapter Four to gain access to different internal areas of the instrument. If you have not already reviewed that chapter, please take the time to do so before diving into a specific corrective procedure.

Also, if you don't find the symptom that you're encountering listed here, you can first take pride in finding a relatively rare problem! But this is as far as pride will take you: you'll then need to either contact me (I will do my best to suggest possibilities) or find a suitable repair person for the job. (I would appreciate hearing about your problem anyway, so I can improve this handbook. I promise to acknowledge your contribution in some potentially embarrassing way!)

Buzzing or Rattling Noises

SYMPTOM: While playing the harmonium, you hear some kind of buzzing or rattling noise, often metallic in nature. Oftentimes you hear the noise only when playing specific notes.

CAUSE: There are generally two sources of buzzing or rattling noises: the harmonium's cover glass or some interference with the free vibration of one or more reeds. (Obviously if your harmonium has no cover glass, it's the reeds.) Cover glass noise usually happens over a broader range of notes than noises caused by the reeds; reed problems usually happen with only one specific note, or with notes that are harmonically sympathetic.

TROUBLESHOOTING/CORRECTING: First remove the cover glass entirely. If this solves the problem, see the procedure below under "Loose Glass." If the noise persists, identify the exact note or notes affected by playing one note at a time. In some cases, you can fix the reed simply by playing it by itself as loud as you can; this might be enough to dislodge small metal burrs that sometimes get stuck around a reed.

Otherwise, you need to identify whether it's the bass or male (or female) reed for the note in question that's having trouble. Push in all the air stops, then pull out only one bass stop. If the same note still rattles, it's the bass reed. Do the same with only one male stop pulled out. On rare occasions you might have trouble with both reeds; you might also have a harmonium in which the air seal between the bass and male reed chambers is weak or nonexistent, in which case this test is not wholly deterministic.

If you want to really be sure that you know which reed is making the noise, remove both the pivot cover and the key for the note in question. Pump the bellows a little to play the note, then stick a small screwdriver down either air hole to prevent that particular reed from vibrating. If the noise stops, you've found your culprit.

In any case, jot down the exact note that's having trouble—A, A#, B ,C, etc. Use sharps to record the note rather than flats because the reeds are internally marked with sharps. Then proceed to the procedure below under "Reed Interference."

OTHER POSSIBILITIES: As harmoniums can produce quite a bit of sound, it's possible that the buzzing or rattling noises (particular softer ones) are coming from another object altogether, such as a nearby window or even another instrument such as a guitar! Perhaps you wear glasses and set them on top of the harmonium while you're playing, and they're bouncing up and down a little. Even a paper clip on the cover glass can make a respectable din!

LOOSE GLASS

The glass in the top cover is not always mounted firmly. The harmonium's sound vibrations may cause this glass to rattle.

If this happens while you are playing and you cannot pause to correct the problem, try holding the glass down with the thumb of your pumping hand. For a more permanent solution, here are a few options:

- Try jiggling the glass in the frame. Often this will fix whatever little rattling there might be.

- Secure the glass in the frame more tightly by wedging little bits of paper or thin cardboard between the glass and the frame.

- For an even more permanent solution, you can remove the glass from the frame, line the inner slots of the frame with a clear glue (such as silicone glue), and reinsert the glass. In some covers, the glass will easily slide out one end of the frame; in others, you may need to pry the frame apart and glue it back together after reinserting the glass.

REED INTERFERENCE

Harmonium owners often think that a loud buzzing or rattling sound means that a reed is broken! But a broken reed makes no sound at all—what's actually happening is that the vibrating reed is making contact with something solid, thereby producing the buzzing or rattling noise.

To correct this problem, you must first ascertain the more specific cause.

Possible Cause #1: *Sunken pivot pin.* Sometimes a key's pivot pin will slip down far enough into the open space where the reed vibrates so that the reed strikes the pin (Figure 5-1; compare with Figure 4-11b, page 81). To see if this is the problem, remove the pivot cover and examine the pivot point of the key in question. A small bit of the pivot pin should stick *above* the key, in which case go

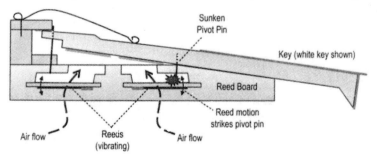

Figure 5-1: Cross-section of a sunken pivot pin hitting a vibrating reed

to #2 below. If you can't see the pin, remove the key itself. If you can see the pin now, use a pair of needle-nose pliers to pull the pin back up then replace the key and the pivot cover. If you can't see the pin, go to #3 below.

Note: if you pull the pin up but it seems to slip too easily back into its hole, you might need to glue the pin in place. (Wait for the glue to dry before re-setting the key!)

There is also the possibility that the vertical guide pin at the back of the keyboard assembly has slipped down. Personally, I've never seen this happen; that pin is set into an extra block of wood and doesn't get the same back-and-forth pressure as the pivot pin. Nevertheless, it is a possibility and would be corrected in the same manner.

Possible Cause #2: *Misaligned reed.* A normal, well-functioning reed, shown in Figure 5-2, has a small gap around the vibrating part of the reed that allows the reed to move up and down without obstruction. If this alignment is

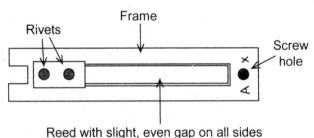

Reed with slight, even gap on all sides

Figure 5-2: A properly aligned reed

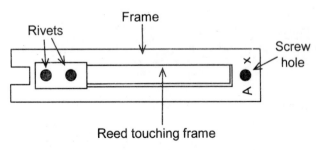

Reed touching frame

Figure 5-3: A misaligned reed

off (Figure 5-3), or if a metal burr is protruding from the frame or the reed, the reed will come in contact with one edge of the frame, thereby producing noise.

To correct these problems, open up the reed chamber and locate the reed in question. The bass reeds are always longer than the male reeds (and usually nearest the keyboard assembly hinges). You'll also see the name of the note written on each reed: *C, Cx* ("x" means sharp), *D, Dx,* etc. You can often verify that you've found the right reed by gently pulling it up a bit on the free end and letting go. A properly aligned reed will vibrate softly; a misaligned reed will definitely rattle.

Once you've located the reed, use a small flathead screwdriver to gently push the free end down into the frame a little bit. You might hear it rubbing on one side of the frame or the other. If it's fairly obvious which side of the reed is rubbing, see if either of these methods corrects the problem:

1. Use your small screwdriver to push the reed through the frame just enough so you can scrape the *frame* with the screwdriver edge (Figure 5-4). This will do a pretty decent job of removing little burrs and such. You might as well scrape all three sides of the frame just to make sure. Note that it's much better to scrape the frame rather than the reed since any change in the amount of material on the reed will slightly alter its pitch.

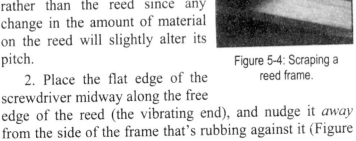

Figure 5-4: Scraping a reed frame.

2. Place the flat edge of the screwdriver midway along the free edge of the reed (the vibrating end), and nudge it *away* from the side of the frame that's rubbing against it (Figure

101

5-5). The reed won't seem to move at all, but it doesn't take much to make the necessary adjustment. Don't worry about being *too* gentle—it needs to be a firm nudge; but don't be overly hard either, as it is possible to break a reed this way (especially an old, brittle one).

Figure 5-5: Nudging a reed

After trying these fixes, flip the keyboard back down and test the note. Don't replace the rear screws yet, though, as you might need to open up again. Instead, use the thumb of your pumping hand to push the keyboard assembly down to make a tight seal.

If the problem persists, double-check that you're really working on the right reed—it's easy to confuse the bass and male reeds when you flip the keyboard upside-down. I've often fiddled for some minutes with one reed only to discover that I was working on the wrong one all along!

If you *are* working the right reed, try repeating the procedures above once more, or you can opt to remove the reed entirely (see page 87) for a closer examination.

With the reed out, hold it up to a light so you can see the gaps on all sides (Figure 5-6). You'll get a good sense of whether the reed is misaligned to one side or the other.

Figure 5-6: Examining the gaps between reed and frame

You can then nudge the reed to the right side, scrape the edges of the frame, or, in the most drastic cases, take a metal file and file away at the frame itself. Again, *don't file the reed,* lest you change its pitch.

The frame's inside corners are a common culprit for reed interference problems. A small, flat file with a square edge will do an excellent job of squaring out these corners (Figure 5-7).

If, after all this, the problem still persists, triple-check that you're really working on the right reed, then try again. Sometimes it just takes patience. In the worst case, you might simply replace the reed altogether.

Figure 5-7: Squaring the reed frame

Possible Cause #3: *Foreign matter.* Occasionally a little bit of material might find its way into the space between the reed and the air hole above it. This might be a wood or metal burr, the bottom end of a pivot pin (or the whole pin itself), or other things like grains of rice from a wedding or a Vedic fire ceremony (I have encountered this). Such material generally bounces up and down on the vibrating reed with no chance of escape.

The obvious correction is to remove the reed and flip the keyboard assembly back over so any such material just falls out.

If you had previously discovered that the pivot pin had sunk far into the reed chamber, removing the reed will allow you to push that pin back to its proper position from the bottom. Again, if the pin slips easily in its hole, you'll want to glue it in place, especially if the wooden reed itself has a split. (See "Loose or Wobbly Keys," page 111.)

Possible Cause #4: *Collision with inside of air hole.* The reed might actually be striking the inside wall of the air hole itself, thereby rattling somewhat. This can happen

103

when environmental conditions cause the wood to expand in some way. This can be tested by pushing the reed into the air hole with a screwdriver and feeling if it hits anything. If it does, remove the reed and gouge away that area of the air hole until the reed can move freely.

Rumbling Noises

SYMPTOM: Rumbling noises are similar to buzzes and rattles but have a different tone quality. They're usually lower-pitched sounds and often occur with multiple adjacent notes.

CAUSE: Some part of the harmonium other than the cover glass is loose and is rattling around. The most common source of this noise is vibration in the lock.

TROUBLESHOOTING/CORRECTING: First try placing a thumb or a knee or something else against the lock. If that stops or diminishes the noise, you might need only to twiddle the lock around to get its pieces set differently. Sometimes a few solid taps will do the trick.

If the lock doesn't seem to be the source, it might be (on a collapsible harmonium) the carrying handle or the pop-out buttons on the sides. On all harmoniums, the source could be a loose piece of ornamental trim. It's also possible that part of the case itself has become loose and is bumping around. You can check for all this by having a friend play the instrument while you place your hands on different parts to see if you can stop the noise.

OTHER POSSIBILITIES: I have encountered harmoniums in which one of the screws holding a reed and its frame to the reed board was broken, thereby causing the reed frame to bounce a little as the reed vibrated. Replacing the screw solved the problem.

Also, if your harmonium is sitting on a table or another piece of furniture, it's possible that a piece of *that* item is rattling. Again, the harmonium produces a lot of vibration and can easily affect other objects around it.

Squeaking Noises

SYMPTOM: You hear a little squeaking or rubbing noise that is either (A) related to specific keys or (B) related to the pumping of the bellows. You can test for the latter by sticking a finger in one of the back valve holes on the external bellows, forcing the valve open. This allows you to move the bellows in and out without building up any air pressure, enabling you to listen to noises related to the motion of the bellows.

CAUSE FOR (A): There is usually a small amount of friction between a key's guide slot and its corresponding vertical guide pin, especially if there's a little sideways pressure on the keys while they're being played. When the inside surface of the key slot has been rubbed and "polished" against the guide pin over time, or when the side of the pin is a little rough, it gets just the right amount of friction to produce a sound not unlike that of a bow against the strings of a violin.

TROUBLESHOOTING/CORRECTING FOR (A): A little graphite on the vertical guide pin can reduce the friction, thereby eliminating the noise. You can also file down the inside of the slot with a thin, flat file (even an emery board), making it just a touch wider so that there's less overall contact between the slot and the pin. Be careful with the file—you don't want to remove so much material that the key becomes wobbly. Also note that the tiny bits of wood that make up the slot are quite fragile—be careful not to break them. If you happen to file off too much material, you can make the pin a little bigger by wrapping a little bit of thin tape around it.

CAUSE FOR (B): If the squeaking noise seems related to the bellows action and not to specific notes, the cause depends on the type of bellows you have. With top-fold bellows, the noise is probably coming from contact between the torsion spring rod (which causes the bellows to open) and the bottom of the bellows. With side-fold bellows, the noise usually comes from contact between the pivot latch and the little nails or screws that protrude from the triangular trim pieces on the corners of the wooden bellows plate.

TROUBLESHOOTING/CORRECTING FOR (B): With top-fold bellows, simply bend the torsion spring rod away from the bellows a little bit to avoid having the two make contact (Figure 5-8). With side-fold bellows, wrap a little bit of electrical tape (more durable than transparent tape) around the top and bottom of the pivot latch. This is generally enough to avoid contact between the latch and the little nails or screws (Figure 5-9).

OTHER POSSIBILITIES: Check to make sure that mice have not infested your harmonium!

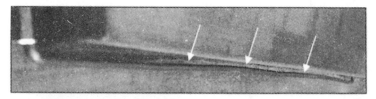

Figure 5-8 (above): Ensure that there's a gap between the torsion rod and the bellows plate with top-fold bellows

Figure 5-9 (left): Creating a small gap between the pivot latch and pieces of trim with a side-fold bellows harmonium

Ticking Noises

SYMPTOM: You hear some kind of a ticking sound that's related to either (A) specific keys as you play them or (B) the pumping action of the bellows. As with the squeaking noises above, you can test for (B) by sticking a finger in the back of the external bellows which allows you to move them in and out without building up air pressure.

CAUSES FOR (A): The key spring may be bumping the cover glass when you press a key. This will happen regardless of whether you're pumping the bellows. If one or more key springs are making contact with the cover glass, you can usually see the glass move a little bit as well. The other possibility is a misalignment of the metal rods that make up the coupler mechanism underneath the key.

TROUBLESHOOTING/CORRECTING FOR (A): If the key springs are making contact, you can either flatten out the offending key springs a little bit or raise the cover glass a little. In the latter case, remove the cover glass and look for a small screw (or nail) on each end of the wooden base for the key springs (Figure 5-10). If you have screws, back them out a half turn or more, thereby lifting the back of the cover glass away from the key springs. If you don't have screws, you can easily add some. Pre-drill holes for the screws if you do this, as the soft wood can easily split otherwise.

Figure 5-10: Cover glass spacer screw

To correct a coupler misalignment, first remove the key that is making the noise. Underneath the key, you'll see the bent ends of a couple of metal rods (Figure 5-11). Notice how they move, and check whether one of the ends makes contact with the other within its range of motion. If this happens, simply bend one or the other rod until they no longer make contact.

Figure 5-11: Misaligned coupler rods (middle) vs. correct position (right)

CAUSES FOR (B): One possibility is that the torsion spring (for top-fold bellows) or the pivot latch (for side-fold bellows) is making some kind of contact with other parts around it. The other possibility is that the internal spring in a side-fold bellows is making contact with itself when compressed.

TROUBLESHOOTING/CORRECTING FOR (B): In the first case, follow the correction procedure for "Squeaking Noises" case (B), page 106. In the latter case, remove the valve on the back of the bellows by removing its screws and gently prying the piece off. Inside the bellows, you'll see a spiral spring fashioned from a metal rod. With the valve off, you can watch the spring being compressed and see where it's touching itself. Then you can bend the spring a little so this no longer happens.

OTHER POSSIBILITIES: Although I don't know of any more specific causes, ticking noises are generally produced by metallic pieces within the instrument rather than wooden ones. This can at least help you narrow down the possibilities.

Leaky Keys

SYMPTOM: A note plays by itself even when its key is not depressed.

CAUSE: When the key is up (in its rest position), its leather seals are not completely shutting off the air holes

108

for its corresponding reeds. The resulting air flow, however slight, allows the reeds to sound.

TROUBLESHOOTING/CORRECTING: Remove the pivot cover, and examine the key and its pivot pin. The key might have popped up and become stuck on the top of the pin such that it's no longer lying flat against the air holes (Figure 5-12). If this is not the case, remove the key and check whether the pivot pin has become bent slightly toward the front of the instrument, in which case the key will be slightly depressed all the time (Figure 5-13).

 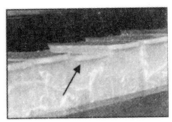

Figure 5-12: A "stuck up" key will draw attention to itself

Figure 5-13: A "depressed" key will always whine a little

Also check the leather seals on the key. If they are not aligned with the edge of the key, trim the protruding edges that might be rubbing against adjacent keys, thereby not allowing the key to fall flat against the air holes. It's good to check the leather on adjacent keys as well, which may be causing the same problem by getting caught underneath the affected key.

OTHER POSSIBILITIES: In older harmoniums, the leather seals may simply be old and brittle so they don't make a very good seal. They can be renewed with a stiff brass-bristle brush or replaced. The wooden part of the key might have become warped such that it doesn't lie flat on top of the air hole. Other than repairing or replacing the key, you can shim the leather by first attaching another piece of leather, then sanding the entire area down at a slight angle so as to compensate for the warp of the key.

Note: If you need to acquire new leather, look specifically for "musical leather," which can be obtained from instrument repair shops or suppliers to such shops.

Sticky Keys

SYMPTOM: Keys don't depress easily or pop up when released.

CAUSE: Something prevents the free motion of the key back to its rest position. This can be a faceplate that is on too tightly, a bent vertical guide or pivot pin (thereby causing too much friction against the key slot on the vertical guide pin), or either splinters or leather seals on the affected key (or adjacent keys) that obstruct the motion.

TROUBLESHOOTING/CORRECTING: First just try vigorously playing the key and its neighbors for a bit. This might loosen things up enough. If the problem persists, check that the faceplate is not rubbing against the keys (see pages 74–75). Then remove the pivot cover and check both the pivot pin and the vertical guide pin, straightening as necessary with needle-nose pliers. You might also file down the key slot a bit as described under "Squeaking Noises" (page 105). If the problem persists, check the leather on the affected key and those adjacent to it as described in "Leaky Keys" (page 108). Also check whether any splinters are protruding between the keys and file them off as necessary.

OTHER POSSIBILITIES: Remember what your mother said about drinking grape juice or eating popsicles while playing the piano? The same applies to the harmonium. If some substance has dropped in between two keys and is causing one or the other to stick, it simply needs to be cleaned off.

As described on page 81 (see Figure 4-12), I've sometimes encountered a key that worked just fine by itself but seemed utterly determined to stick while playing certain pieces on the harmonium. What I eventually found was that when I played the particular key, I was putting a little sideways pressure on it. This caused it to rub against an adjacent key that I played next. With this second key down and the first rubbing against it, the first didn't want to spring back up. In this case, one can either adjust one's playing style or opt—as I did—to fix the key as described in the next section.

Loose or Wobbly Keys

SYMPTOM: A key moves side to side to a greater extent than other keys; this is often a lateral rotation of the key in relation to its centerline (Figure 5-14). This doesn't necessarily affect the sound (unless it's causing the key to stick) but is somewhat uncomfortable to play.

CAUSE: A key's side to side motion is restricted by both the pivot pin and the vertical guide pin at the back of the key. If the pivot pin is sunken or

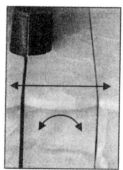

Figure 5-14: Motions of a wobbly key

loose, if the pivot cover is not on tightly enough, or if one side of the guide slot has cracked, the key will become wobbly.

TROUBLESHOOTING/CORRECTING: If multiple keys are loose or wobbly, first check that the pivot cover is tightened down fully. This doesn't mean that it's really tight against the keys—there is always a little space to allow the keys to pivot.

If only a single key is loose, remove the pivot cover and examine the pivot pin more carefully. If the pin has sunk a little, it won't be properly restricting the key's rotation; in this case, simply remove the key and pull the pin back up with needle-nose pliers. (You might want to glue it in place if it seems too slippery, as described earlier under "Reed Interference," pages 99–100.)

If the pin height looks fine, wobble the key a little side to side and see whether the pivot pin wobbles too. It shouldn't! But if it does, the hole in which the pin sits is too wide. In this case, you'll need to either glue the pin or tighten the pin in the hole some other way (such as filling the hole with putty and redrilling it to a smaller size). I have encountered situations in which the reed board itself had split directly through one of these holes, thereby expanding it slightly. In this case, it is necessary to glue the pin—and the split, for that matter!

If everything around the pivot pin looks fine, remove the key and see whether one side of the slot around the vertical guide pin is loose or otherwise damaged. Too much vigorous pounding on a key can weaken and break these little bits of wood, which will then cease to keep the key steady. In many cases you can glue or otherwise reinforce the slot; in extreme cases you may need to rebuild or replace the entire key.

It may be that the slot is simply too wide. In this case, try wrapping a layer of transparent tape around one side of the slot or around the guide pin. You might also paint a thin layer of all-purpose glue on one side of the slot (let it to dry before reinstalling the key, of course).

OTHER POSSIBILITIES: Although I haven't encountered this, it's possible that the vertical guide pin itself is loose, in which case it needs to be stiffened as appropriate.

"Wheezing"

SYMPTOM: The harmonium just doesn't seem to have any "umph" in its overall sound, or it seems as though you have to pump an awful lot more than you used to, or you notice that the instrument doesn't play as well relative to other harmoniums of the same size (not larger ones). The harmonium might also not have much sustaining capability, meaning that the sound dies off quickly after you stop pumping the external bellows.

CAUSE: The harmonium isn't internally retaining enough air to produce a steady, pleasant sound. The air might be leaking through old or faulty seals. The bellows, internal or external, might have leaks, they might be stiff, or the springs that push against the internal bellows are either too weak or too strong. Another possibility for leaking bellows is that the leather flap inside the rear valve on the external bellows has become curled such that it no longer seals off the air holes on the rear valve when you compress the bellows.

TROUBLESHOOTING/CORRECTING: First check the rear valve on the external bellows (see Figure 4-7, page 78)—if you can feel air blowing out the back when you compress the bellows, you definitely need to remove the rear valve and massage the leather flat again so it seals properly (Figure 5-15).

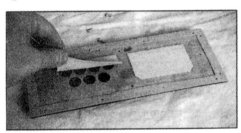

Figure 5-15: Rear flap valves. These should naturally lay flat to function properly

Otherwise, check next for other leaks around the edges of the external bellows. Move the key spring for one key aside (as in Figure 2-11, page 33) so that you can continuously pump with one hand while feeling for air around the bellows with your other hand. Wet lips are also quite sensitive to blowing air and are a good way to feel for leaks.

If you find a leak, you'll need to patch it in some way. Leaks where the bellows meet the harmonium case can be filled in with a strong glue. Leaks in the leather and cardboard areas of the bellows are best patched from the inside, which you can get to by removing the rear valve cover. With a side-fold bellows, you might also need to temporarily remove the inner spring.

Once inside, you can glue pieces of thin leather or other nonporous material (even paper) against the leaky area. If the rupture is significant, you might need to replace or rebuild the bellows. (This necessitates cutting them off the main body of the instrument altogether.) When attaching repaired or new bellows, be sure to use a strong glue (rather than an all-purpose glue).

If you don't have any external leaks, *listen* for internal ones next. In a quiet room, pump the external bellows a few times *without holding any keys down* to build some internal pressure. Then stop pumping and just listen. If you hear any significant hissing or wheezing (very minor hissing is not a problem), pump a little more and listen again while moving around the instrument to hear exactly where it's coming from. It might be coming through the top, or you might hear it more through the sides. In any case, you'll get a good sense of where to look before diving in.

Hissing sounds that come from the top or from the upper half of the instrument are probably related to the seals between the reed board and the upper assembly (refer to Figure 4-18 on page 85). Open up the reed chamber, and brush away any bits of material (typically sawdust) that are stuck into the leather. (Even tiny bits can produce a small leak.) It's also a good idea to renew the leather with a brass-bristle brush.

Also check that the seals are actually attached all the way around (you'll accomplish this by brushing them), including the seal that directs air to the internal bellows. If any are loose, glue them back down, and make sure that there are no gaps between the leather and the wood or between different pieces of leather. The most insidious leaks are those in which there's only a small lapse in the glue. Here you may need to peel back more of the leather in order to glue the particular spot in question. Of course, you can be creative and blob some glue on the inside of the leak, close the harmonium, then pump a bit to push the glue into the hole.

If you hear hissing lower down in the instrument, you might have a leak in the internal bellows. In this case, you will need to disassemble the whole instrument to examine and repair them as necessary.

If you don't hear any leaks, but the instrument is still wheezing, you can try playing around with the inner bellows and their springs. Sometimes the inner bellows are just a bit stiff—they might never have been fully expanded since they were made. In this case, detach the stop board and pull up and down enough to flex the bellows a few times (if they're attached) or pull them out entirely and stretch them out with your hands.

The tension of the inner springs can affect your harmonium's performance. If they are too strong, they never allow much air to accumulate in the inner bellows. If they are too weak, they won't push all the air out. In either case, the air flow is restricted. You can strengthen the springs by stretching them out a bit. Similarly, you can weaken them by bending them such that they are more compressed in their natural state.

OTHER POSSIBILITIES: Advise your harmonium to quit smoking. Just kidding. Of course, if it's always played around large-scale Vedic fire ceremonies (like one I attended at a mountaintop temple in India, where the whole room was filled with smoke from the gallons of oiled herbs that we'd thrown into a fire pit), this may be unavoidable!

On a more serious note, it may also simply be a matter of one's personal playing style—timid pumping of the external bellows generally produces a weak sound. Allow the external bellows to open more each time you pump them, thereby increasing the air flow through the instrument. It might help to adjust the external bellows spring so that the bellows will open up more on their own. On a top-fold bellows, this means increasing the twist in the torsion spring rod at the bottom of the bellows. On a side-fold model, this means removing the inner spring and stretching it out a little more.

Slow, Fast, or Non-Sounding Notes

SYMPTOM: Relative to other notes, certain notes respond more slowly, more quickly, or not at all.

CAUSE: A reed produces sound by being momentarily bent in one direction by the flow of air, then springing back in the opposite direction for a bit before being pushed by the air again. To initially bend the reed takes more energy—that is, a stronger push of air—than to simply keep it moving. Thus, a reed must be positioned in its frame such that it takes neither too little nor too much air to start it moving. If a reed is not so positioned it will sound either too quickly or too slowly, or possibly not at all. It's also possible that a reed has simply become stuck.

TROUBLESHOOTING/CORRECTING: A properly aligned reed sits just above its frame, essentially parallel to the frame itself (Figure 5-16). Maladjusted reeds might be slightly above or below this level. The father away the reed is from this position, the more it will be noticeably different from others.

Whether a reed is slow or fast really makes no difference (although slow is the more common condition). If the reed is bent too far into the frame, gently bend it out; if it's

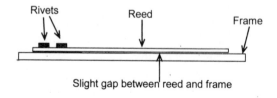

Figure 5-16: Proper vertical alignment of a reed

too far out, gently bend it in. Either adjustment is best done when looking at the reed itself. To bend the reed out, slip a thin screwdriver or knife underneath it and tug it up from the frame a few times, then check the result and repeat if needed. To bend a reed in, simply push on it with a thin screwdriver a few times, check, and repeat as needed.

A quick fix for a slow reed (which is typically too far into the frame) is to remove the pivot cover and the affected key, then poke a narrow screwdriver down the air hole to bend the reed out a little bit (Figure 5-17).

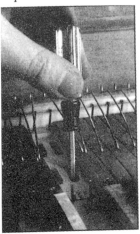

If a reed isn't making any sound at all, it's probably jammed against the wall of the air hole above which it's mounted. In this case you will need to widen the air hole slightly (it might have expanded as a result of environmental factors) until the reed can move freely again.

Figure 5-17: Quick-fixing a slow reed from above

OTHER POSSIBILITIES: The higher a reed's pitch, the shorter and stiffer it is from the outset and the less responsive it generally is to the flow of air. Very high-pitched reeds just don't sound easily at all, and there's little one can do without having to risk breaking the reed in the process. In such cases, it's good to have a spare set of reeds!

Out-of-Tune Notes

SYMPTOM: One or more notes are out of tune with the rest of the instrument, or the whole instrument is out of tune with standard-tuned references.

CAUSE: Any number of conditions can change the flexibility and weight distribution in a reed, thereby altering its pitch. These include dirt, corrosion, and other deposits; aging; or simply the fact that the instrument wasn't tuned properly to begin with. Brass reeds also become more brittle as they age, raising their pitch—I worked over one 60+-year-old harmonium that had gone uniformly sharp by almost a half-step! Deposits and manufacturing defects, on the other hand, can make individual reeds either sharp or flat.

TROUBLESHOOTING/CORRECTING: When you have determined which reeds are affected, open up the reed chamber and take a look at them. If you see any dirt or other deposits, clean them off and check the tuning again. This might be a sufficient correction. If the reed looks clean, it needs more precise tuning.

Tuning a Harmonium

A harmonium is tuned by tuning its individual reeds. Tuning a reed involves adding or removing material from either its base or its tongue. Simply said, if the reed is made to vibrate more quickly, it will sound a higher pitch; if it is made to vibrate more slowly, it will sound lower. But before looking at specific methods for this, a few helpful notes are in order.

HELPFUL HINTS

Tuning reeds is most easily done with some kind of "needle" tuner (physical or simulated with an LCD) that tells you exactly how *far* out of tune a reed happens to be, rather than the mere fact that it's out of tune. Knowing the extent of the necessary tuning helps you determine how much material should be added or removed.

Most harmoniums seem to be tuned to a standard A of 444 Hz or 445 Hz rather than 440 Hz. This is not because they use a different tuning fork in India. (The folks at Bina assured me they don't.) I figure that it's because most Indian harmoniums are manufactured and initially tuned in an environment of 95 degrees/90+ percent humidity. When these instruments are later played in cooler and drier climates (such as in Seattle, where the temperature is easily 30 degrees lower most of the time), they seem to be about 1 percent sharp. A possible explanation is that the reeds become more flexible when heated, and vibrate slower in thicker air.

Whatever the reason, it's helpful before tuning individual reeds to have a tuner that can be calibrated for a standard A of 444–445 Hz, or whatever the harmonium in question seems to have as a baseline. Also, if the harmonium is being played with other instruments (guitars, flutes, violins, and so on), you might be tempted to tune the whole instrument to 440 Hz in whatever environment you happen to have. There's no problem with this other than that it's a *lot* of work to tune an entire harmonium (close to 80 individual reeds) and that most other instruments can be tuned on the spot anyway. My recommendation, then, is to get the harmonium in tune with itself and resort to a complete tuning only if the instrument is systematically out of tune to a significant degree (like the antique I mentioned earlier).

It's worth mentioning that there are different ways to tune a harmonium relative to itself. The simplest way (and the only way in which this author has any experience) is to tune each reed in turn against a tuner. The more classical and professional way involves listening to and counting beats between specific pairs of notes. Specific details can be found in *The American Reed Organ and the Harmonium* by Robert Gellerman.

As a practical matter, it's more convenient to check the tuning of all of the reeds at once, then open up the harmonium, adjust the necessary reeds, and check the whole thing again. Otherwise, you're constantly flipping the keyboard assembly up and down all the time, which gets really tiresome. For this purpose, it's helpful to have a tuning sheet like that in Appendix C (page 147), where you can write down how much tuning is needed on each reed.

INDIVIDUAL REED TUNING

Again, tuning a reed means either adding or removing material from its base or its tongue:

Raising the pitch of a reed involves either *adding* material to the **base**—making it stiffer—or *removing* material from the **tongue**—making it lighter.

Lowering the pitch of a reed involves either *removing* material from the **base**—making it more flexible—or *adding* material to the **tongue**—making it heavier.

These are principles that have been known from the earliest days of free-reed instruments. As mentioned in Chapter One, historians say that the ancient peoples of Asia tuned the reeds of their mouth-organs with small blobs of wax. The technology hasn't changed much in several millennia!

Removing material can be done with a small file, a sharp knife (as I watched folks at Bina use in their factory), or a special reed-scraping tool while one holds the free end of the reed in some way to keep it firm (for example, a flathead screwdriver under the free end of an *in-situ* reed, or your finger with a loose reed). You then scrape away small portions of brass (Figure 5-18). **CAUTION:** the smaller the reed, the thinner the material; the older the reed, the more brittle it is—be very careful in these cases, lest you break the reed.

How much material to remove (at either base or tongue) depends on how far you need to tune the reed and the on size of the reed itself. The larger the reed, the more material must be removed for the same degree of tuning relative to a small reed. There is nothing better here than

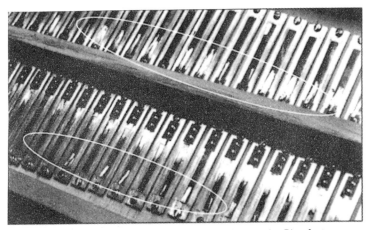

Figure 5-18: Scraping marks from tuning done at the Bina factory

giving yourself some time for experimentation as well as self-forgiveness. Remove only small amounts at first, then check the result. Soon you'll get a feel for the process. After a while, you'll probably find yourself gouging away at a stubborn reed that just doesn't want to get in tune. Of course, be sure that you're working on the same reed that you're checking with the tuner! (This suggestion comes from direct experience.)

Adding material can be done in a variety of ways. If you want to play with the ancients, you can certainly use bits of wax. However, I imagine that wax tends to fall off occasionally, which wouldn't be my first choice during a performance of some kind! Thus I've generally opted for other more modern and more persistent substances: all-purpose glue (that is, Elmer's) and/or masking tape (Figure 5-19, next page).

Small drops of glue (applied with a toothpick) make a good, permanent material: once dry, such glue will not absorb much ambient moisture and will not change much over time. On the downside, however, you have to wait some twelve hours for the glue to dry (that is, lose all its water) before you can check the results. This obviously

Figure 5-19: Tuning reeds with masking tape and glue. The dried glue is visible on the right side of those reeds that don't have tape on them.

This particular harmonium, which is a few decades old, was fairly sharp across the board and required considerable tuning. You can see that I did some scraping at the base of most of these reeds in addition to adding weight to their tongues.

makes the process somewhat tedious; I imagine you could use a hair dryer to speed the process; if you do, wait for the reeds to cool back down to the ambient air temperature before checking their tuning.

The other difficulty with glue is that if you overshoot your tuning and add too much, it's difficult to remove a little bit once the glue is dry. A number of times I tried to cut a little bit of glue away, only to detach the whole blob.

I've also found that since Elmer's glue is mostly water, the amount of dry material that you actually build up is a lot less than it looked like when you applied the wet stuff. For this reason, I've thought to mix brass filings into the glue, to add more weight with a smaller blob. I have not yet tried this technique, however.

Adding tiny strips of masking tape, on the other hand, lets you check the results immediately. For this I like to take a strip of ¾-inch tape cut in half lengthwise. I place this strip on some part of the reed board that's not used for anything and cut off one millimeter wide bits with an X-acto knife. This size seems to fit on most of the reeds, even the high ones (which are very narrow). The only potential downside to this method is that the tape will probably become brittle over time and might fall off in 10 years or so. Nevertheless, it's much faster than using glue and has good longevity.

As a final note, you might play around a little with how the two reeds for the same note are tuned relative to one another, as well as relative to the reeds an octave above and below. Part of the charm of a harmonium's overall sound is that it's not 100 percent perfectly in tune with itself. Slight variations between the reeds for the same note create, in large part, a specific instrument's "character." You don't necessarily want that character to be too straightlaced nor too predictable. Like a good friend or partner, personality quirks are what make them special! Indeed, are not those very quirks what we love most deeply in others?

Vive la différence!

Air Stops, Drones, and Tremolo Knobs for Select Bina Harmoniums

(Knobs are numbered left to right)

MODELS 8, 9, 11, AND 12 (STANDARD, SEVEN KNOBS)

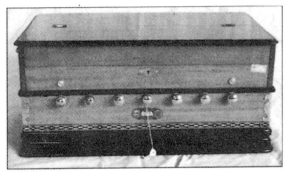

1: Air stop, male reeds   5: Tremolo
2: Drone   6: Drone
3: Air stop, bass reeds   7: Air stop, male reeds
4: Drone

MODEL 2½ OCTAVE TK (STANDARD, FOUR KNOBS)

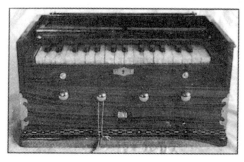

1: Air stop, male reeds   3: Tremolo (or drone)
2: Air stop, bass reeds   4: Drone (or tremolo)

MODEL 23B 3¼ OCTAVE (COLLAPSIBLE, SIX KNOBS)

1: Air stop, male reeds   4: Drone
2: Air stop, bass reeds   5: Tremolo
3: Air stop, bass reeds   6: Drone

MODEL 23B 2½ OCTAVE
(COLLAPSIBLE, FOUR KNOBS)

1: Air stop, male reeds   3: Tremolo

2: Air stop, bass reeds   4: Drone

MODELS 13, 15, 17, 30B, "SWAR" AND "SANGEET"
(STANDARD, NINE KNOBS)
ALSO MODEL 23B 3½ OCTAVE
(COLLAPSIBLE, NINE KNOBS)

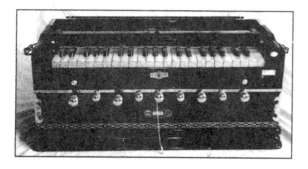

1: Air stop, male reeds   6: Drone
2: Drone   7: Tremolo
3: Air stop, bass reeds   8: Drone
4: Drone   9: Air stop, male reeds
5: Air stop, bass reeds

Chords and Chord Inversions

Any given chord of three notes has three different *inversions* or ways of fingering that chord. The inversions for every major and minor chord are given later in this appendix.

In each chord, there is a low (or root) note—the one corresponding to the name of the chord—a middle note, and a high note.* The *root* chord is that in which the low note is the same as the name of the chord. The root C major chord, for instance, has the notes C-E-G (from left to right, Figure B-1a); a root G major chord has the notes G-B-D (Figure B-1b).

Figure B-1a: Root C major chord

Figure B-1b: Root G major chord

---

*The number of half-steps between these notes differentiates major, minor, diminished, and augmented chords. A major chord has four half-steps between the root and middle notes and three between the middle and high. A minor chord goes three-four, a diminished chord three-three, and an augmented chord four-four.

The *first inversion* of a chord occurs when the original low note becomes the high note (and the original middle note the new low note). The first inversion of the C chord is E-G-C; that of G is B-D-G (see Figures B-2a and B-2b).

Figure B-2a: First inversion of the C major chord

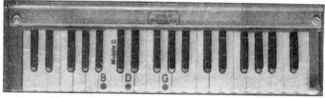

Figure B-2b: First inversion of the G major chord

The *second inversion* of a chord occurs when the original high note becomes the low note (and the original middle note the new high note), as in G-C-E (C chord, Figure B-3a) and D-G-B (G chord, Figure B-3b).

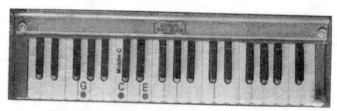

Figure B-3a: Second inversion of the C major chord

Figure B-3b: Second inversion of the G major chord

Given that you have three possible ways to play any given chord, you can simplify many chord transitions. Switching between the root forms of C and G, for instance, requires a significant change in hand position. Switching between the root form of C (Figure B-1a) and the *first* inversion of G (Figure B-2b), on the other hand, means that you can keep the little finger on the G note and simply move the lower fingers between C-E and B-D pairs (see Figure B-4a).* The same works for the *second* inversion of C (one octave down, as in Figure B-3a) and the *root* form of G (Figure B-1b), wherein you can keep your thumb on the G and use your upper fingers to switch (again) between C-E and B-D pairs (as shown in Figure B-4b).

Figure B-4a: Switching between a root C chord and the first inversion of G

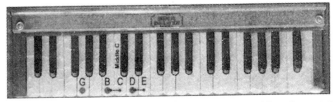

Figure B-4b: Switching between the second inversion of C and a root G

Being a little familiar with inversions especially helps you make smoother transitions between chords that share no common notes—you can find combinations wherein the

---

*One way to play this is with the thumb on B, the index finger on C, the middle finger on D, the ring finger on E, and the little finger on G. This allows you to switch between C and G chords simply by switching fingers. If also playing F chords, as is common with C and G, I find it helpful to keep the ring finger on F, the middle finger on E, the index finger on D, and switch between B and C with the thumb.

two fingers you aren't using for one chord can play two of the notes in the other chord, leaving you with only one finger that has to switch between two notes itself (which is what often produces a choppiness in the sound).

Figure B-5 shows such a transition between G (first inversion, shown with small dots) and F (second inversion, shown with large dots). In this transition, the thumb moves from the B to the A. You lift the middle finger and little finger off the D and G notes (in the G chord) while pressing down the index finger and the ring finger (not used in the G chord) on the C and F notes, respectively.

Figure B-5: A smooth transition between G and F chords

Chord Inversion Diagrams

For each basic major and minor chord, the following pages show which keys on the harmonium keyboard make up the root chord, the first inversion, and the second inversion. The specific configurations shown here are generally those that work the best with the harmonium, being neither too high nor too low for vocal accompaniment. Thus, in some cases, the particular chord may be shown an octave above or below its related chords.

C MAJOR

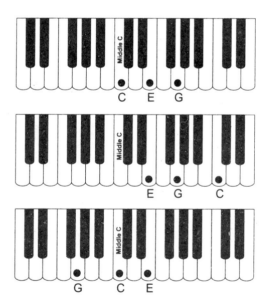

C[#] Major/ D^b Major

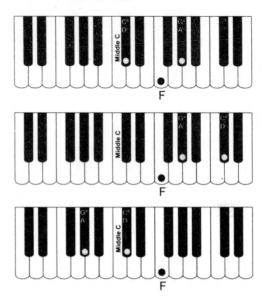

D Major

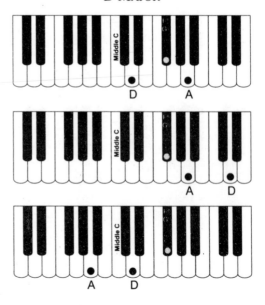

D# Major/Eb Major

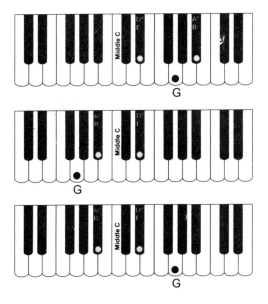

E Major

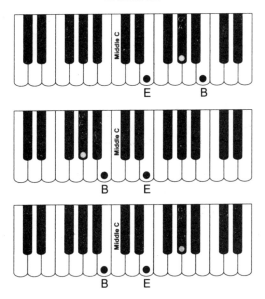

F Major

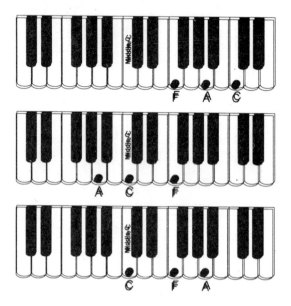

F# Major/Gb Major

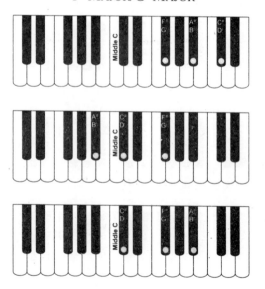

G Major

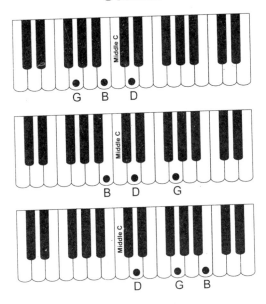

G# Major/Ab Major

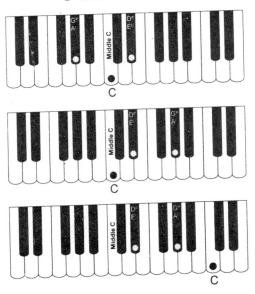

A Major

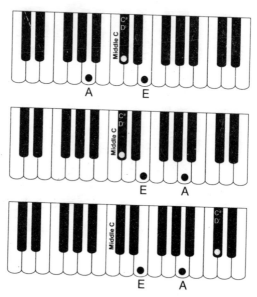

A# Major/B♭ Major

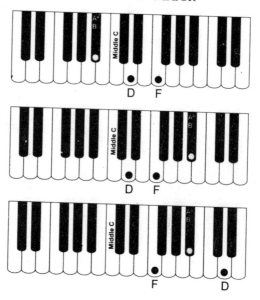

B MAJOR

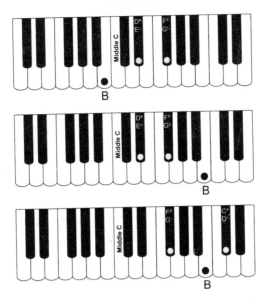

A MINOR

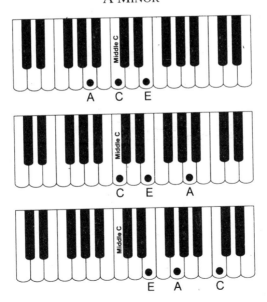

A# Minor/Bb Minor

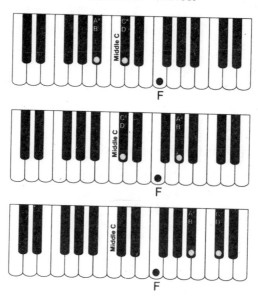

B Minor

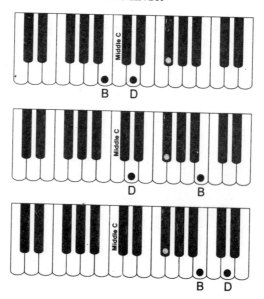

C Minor

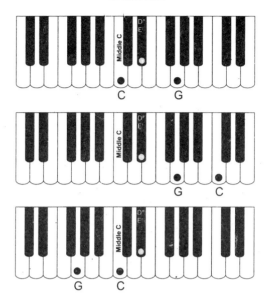

C# Minor/Db Minor

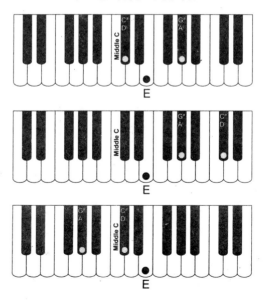

D MINOR

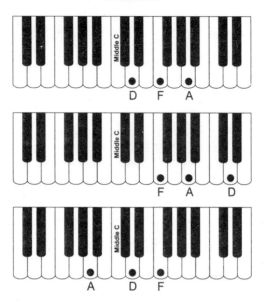

D# MINOR/Eb MINOR

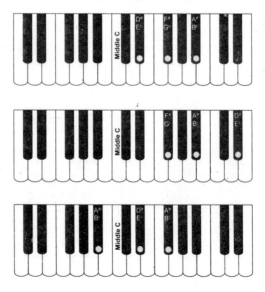

E MINOR

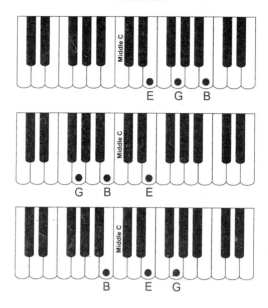

F MINOR

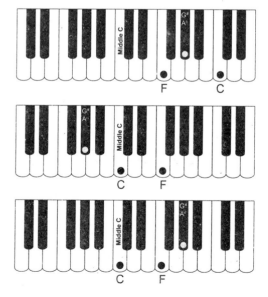

F[#] Minor/G^b Minor

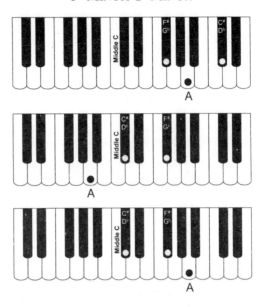

G Minor

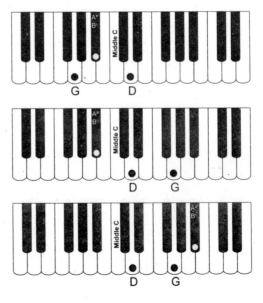

G$^\#$ MINOR/A$^\flat$ MINOR

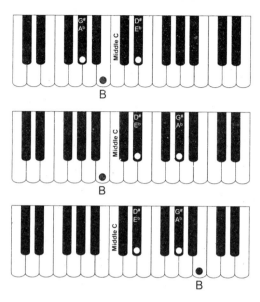

—Appendix C—

Harmonium Tuning Sheet

The sheets on the following two pages can be photo-copied for your personal or professional use in tuning harmoniums. Both sheets (one for male reeds, the other for bass reeds) cover 4 octaves, so you won't necessarily use all the spaces.

For each note in the first, second, third, and fourth octaves, there are several spaces in which you can write the number of "cents" that a reed is out of tune, such as +23 or -17. With this, you can check each reed in turn with a tuner and write down the offset. Then you can open the harmonium, work on the reeds, and check the tuning again, writing the numbers down in the next space.

If a reed is in tune, you can place a check mark in the space or circle the note name to so indicate. Otherwise, open the harmonium again and tune the necessary reeds.

Most reeds can be tuned in one to three attempts. With practice, you'll also develop a feel for how much to work on different reeds, depending on their relative sizes and how much tuning is necessary.

Tuning Sheet—Male Reeds

Note	1st	2nd	3rd	4th	Note	1st	2nd	3rd	4th
C-1					C-3				
C#-1					C#-3				
D-1					D-3				
D#-1					D#-3				
E-1					E-3				
F-1					F-3				
F#-1					F#-3				
G-1					G-3				
G#-1					G#-3				
A-1					A-3				
A#-1					A#-3				
B-1					B-3				
C-2					C-4				
C#-2					C#-4				
D-2					D-4				
D#-2					D#-4				
E-2					E-4				
F-2					F-4				
F#-2					F#-4				
G-2					G-4				
G#-2					G#-4				
A-2					A-4				
A#-2					A#-4				
B-2					B-4				

Tuning Sheet—Bass Reeds

Note	1st	2nd	3rd	4th	Note	1st	2nd	3rd	4th
C-1					C-3				
C#-1					C#-3				
D-1					D-3				
D#-1					D#-3				
E-1					E-3				
F-1					F-3				
F#-1					F#-3				
G-1					G-3				
G#-1					G#-3				
A-1					A-3				
A#-1					A#-3				
B-1					B-3				
C-2					C-4				
C#-2					C#-4				
D-2					D-4				
D#-2					D#-4				
E-2					E-4				
F-2					F-4				
F#-2					F#-4				
G-2					G-4				
G#-2					G#-4				
A-2					A-4				
A#-2					A#-4				
B-2					B-4				

INDEX

accidentals, 59, 68, 71

adjustments. *See* malfunctions

Aeolo-melodicon, early reed organ, 12

air flow, sustaining. *See* playing

air stops, 30-31, 34, 85, 87

Amazing Grace, song, 33

American Reed Organ and the Harmonium, The, 22, 32n, 119

Art and Science of Raja Yoga, The, 22

Audion Piano, precursor to electronic keyboards, 17

Autobiography of a Yogi, 20, 21n

Awaken to Superconsciousness, 22

bassoon, 9

beating-reed instruments, 9

Bell, Alexander Graham, 16

bellows: top-fold (also double-fold, triple fold), 27, 77; side-fold (also multi-fold), 28, 78; inner, 28–29, 86, accessing, 89–91; inner spring, 28; operation of 28–30, 47–48, 91–93; leaks in and repairs, 30, 113–114; cleaning, 30; draining air pressure, 38; operation of stiffness while pumping, 48; robustness, 50; use as a drum, 69n; valves, 86, 105, 107, 113. *See also* pumping *and* springs, bellows

Berner, Alfred, author, 17

bhajans, recordings of, 70

Bina, harmonium manufacturer, 32, 35, 79, 118; models and configurations: #8, 125; #9, 125, #11, 125; #12, 125; #13, 127; #15, 127; #17, 127; #23B (3¼ and 2½ octave), 85, 126, 3½ octave, 127; #30B, 127; 2½ TK, 125; Swar, 127; Sangeet, 127.

Black Swan Inn, New Hampshire, 14

bleating, as of sheep, c.f. 64

Brahms, Johannes, c.f. 26

buzzing noises. *See* malfunctions

Carnegie Hall, New York, 21n

chanting: devotional, 19, 21, 22, 55; leading with voice, 58; for a group, 59; sources of music, 70. *See also* melody, harmony, rhythm, *and* tempo

Chants and Prayers, recording, 70

chants (of Paramhansa Yogananda): *O God Beautiful,* 21n; *Door of My Heart,* 56–58, 59–61, 65; *Listen, Listen, Listen,* 65; *I Will Sing Thy Name,* 69, 71

China, 9, 18

chords: 52, 55, 66; harmonies with, 62; discordant, 62; fingering for, 63–67, 131–132 (transitions), 133–145 (diagrams); trios, 64–65; intervals, 66, 129n; roots and inversions, 129–145; diminished and augmented, 129n

clarinet, 9

Classical Squeezebox, The, 13

cleaning, 39–40

BOOKS OF RELATED INTEREST FROM NAB

SELF-TRANSFORMATION THROUGH MUSIC— *Joanne Crandall*
The power of music to influence us is extraordinary. And this mysterious quality of harmony reacts alike on the composer, the musician, and the listener. In this self-help book of theory and practical exercises, the author explains how we can put music to good use in our daily life; actually making it a part of our living experience; let it penetrate our soul so that we truly become one with the tones, rhythm, harmonics, the cadence of the music we are composing, or playing, or to which we are listening.

ISBN: 81-7822-024-5

SINGING BOWLS: A Practical Handbook of Instruction and Use—*Eva Rudy Jansen*
Singing bowls and ritual objects of Tibet have sound therapeutic value also besides being used in meditation, healing and prayer. The author discusses the meeting between East and West, singing bowls, sacrificial dishes, how the bowls work, synchronization and inner massage, shamanism and brainwaves, and practical instruction for working with these sounds. It provides practical information about using them as well as showing you how to go about finding the bowl that is right for you.

ISBN: 81-7822-103-9

STOLEN SUNSHINE: A Woman's Quest for Herself — *Smita Jhavar*
Set in pre-independence and post-independence scenarios, *Stolen Sunshine* delves into delicate inter-personal relationships in a typical traditional family and each girl's individual reaction to the same situation. Radha rejects her mother's religious beliefs, but succumbs to tradition. Her daughters—Krishna toes the line like her mother and Rukmini manoeuvres her way to find a place for herself in a society dominated by traditions, religion, dogmas, values and elders. Is she accepted by the household and the society?

ISBN: 81-7822-080-6

INDIAN BOOK SHELF
LONDON WIT 5NW (U.K.)
Ph. : (020) 7380 0622
E-mail : indbooks@aol.com

£ 5-95

stops, drone. *See* drones and drone
   reeds
storage, 43

temperature, effects, 40-42
tempo, effects, 54
tremolo, 31, 32–33, 34 , 85, 87
troubleshooting. *See* malfunctions
tuner, electronic, 118, 147
tuning. *See* reeds, tuning

Uranion, early reed organ, 12

valves, bellows. *See* bellows, valves
vibrato, 32
vina, 9
Vivekananda, Swami, 21
Volger, Georg Joseph, 12
Volger's Orchestrion, 12

Walters, J. Donald, 22, 70;
   recordings of, 70
warbling. *See* pumping
Wave of the Sea, source of chant
   music, 61, 70
"wheezer" and "wheezing" 30, 42,
   43, 86, 96, 112–114

yakisoba, non-relation to author,
   159n
Yogananda, Paramhansa. *See*
   Paramhansa Yogananda